HOW A WORLD TEACHER COMES

AS SEEN BY ANCIENT AND MODERN PSYCHOLOGY

FOUR LECTURES DELIVERED AT THE QUEEN'S HALL, LONDON,
DURING JUNE AND JULY: 1926

BY

ANNIE BESANT

A Yesterday's World Publishing

Published by A Yesterday's World Publishing
Copyright © 2019 A Yesterday's World Publishing
First impression 2019
ISBN - 978-1-912925-32-2

LECTURE I

FRIENDS:—

As you know, this is the first of four lectures that I am to give on successive Sundays in this hall, having as the general title announces, the World Teacher regarded or studied, I do not quite remember which word is used, from Eastern and Western Psychology.

I propose this evening to give what I may call an introductory lecture, touching on points of supreme importance from my own standpoint as regards what I am to say to you about this coming of the Teacher. And I will ask you to remember that it is a subject that I have been dealing with now for many years, have lectured on in country after country, including last year, after the course was over, the special lecture given on this subject, printed so that you can read it. Now in all those lectures I based the subject very, very largely on the fact that in the previous comings of the World-Teacher you might trace in history a particular sequence. So that I shall only just allude, in passing, to the fact that His coming in the past has been accompanied by the appearance of a new type of mankind. I am not going to speak about that now, but I mention the fact, and also of the founding of a new civilisation specially intended for the evolution of that new type. My appeal in those lectures was for study, that if you thought that in what I said I had made out a certain case worthy of consideration, then you could study it for yourselves, and on that study base any opinion that might appeal to you, for or against my argument.

During these lectures I shall follow a different line, the line of psychology. But that also will be a line that you can study and criticise for yourselves, points on which you can judge as well as any one else can, and agree or differ from my conclusions according to your judgment.

For I hold that the work of a speaker on a public platform is not to provide his audience with ready-made opinions, but rather to say what he believes to be true, to give the evidence which has convinced himself of the truth, and then to leave every member to judge for himself as to the value of what has been said. I have often compared myself to a signpost, a signpost at the corner of a road which points in a particular direction, but I have never pretended that my walking on the road ought to make you walk upon it, if you do not want to. Nor have I ever said that if you wanted to reach the town or the place that it was enough for me to walk along the road while you stood where you were: a man has to walk the road of Truth for himself, and no one else can do it for him. But one may be able to point to evidence to be studied, to give some suggestions that may be helpful.

In all these lectures I have only put forward the views I came to and the evidence that I used as my own justification, and not as any claim to dictate to anyone of you what you should think. And I am in honour bound to do that, because I belong to a Society whose members are left free on every point to which they choose to turn their thought, and there is no one in the Society, from the oldest to the youngest member, who has any right to dictate to any other member of the Theosophical Society what he shall believe. That is his own duty, and his own responsibility. I have said that over and over again, but I say it all the more emphatically in regard to the lecture I am going to give, because in that I am going to travel into regions in which many of you may not have had experience. I am not going to deal with history or psychology; I am going to put to you certain things

1

which I believe to be true; I go further, I know them to be true. But that is no reason why you should accept them, for the testimony of one person to a truth, or of a few persons to a truth little known or studied, has no valid authority except for themselves. Hence, it is perhaps specially my duty to say that you must not think the Society is in any way responsible for what I say; I am responsible. You can judge it exactly as you please.

This evening I am going to deal with certain matters that I assert to be facts within my own knowledge, and my own experience. Some of these have as their basis facts of the invisible world, which are expounded in all the great religions. All the great religions have their books, and those who wrote them have long passed away. Those that I am going to put to you—though they may be paralleled from those books, specially from those of the Hindus and Buddhists—deal very, very much with the worlds invisible, how to reach them, how to remember experiences there, and so on. But those books have a certain authority, because they are received by millions of people, and in that way there may be a kind of background of authority for some of the facts, as I allege them, that I am going to give to you now. But, on the other hand, I think it would be well for you to remember, anyhow I put it to you as a thing you ought to remember, that whenever anyone travels into a land not known to any of his contemporaries he brings back his own experiences; they are derided, very often put aside as travellers' tales. Supposing he has been accurate in his statements, then others who travel to that same country may have similar experiences, and bring back similar records of their observations. And there is one that I mentioned the other day in speaking on this subject, that the older amongst you will remember, for I read about it and heard it talked about when I was very young, and that was the first great journey made into Central Africa, made by the Frenchman, de Chaillu. He brought back some very extraordinary things as to what he saw there, many of which have been confirmed and are now accepted. But I remember one which made an impression upon my young imagination, it was that of the gorilla: the terrible creature who reared on his hind legs, struck his chest with his arms, and so on. He was very much laughed at, and told such creatures were impossible, told he was frightened, ran away, and did not examine the animal. But many people here have seen a gorilla, and you know that de Chaillu was justified in the description he gave of that very unpleasant animal. Similarly, if I am to speak of worlds which you have not visited, or come back without a memory of what you have seen and heard, it may seem strange to you, and unusual. But, after all, that is the case with all the statements made in the great Scriptures of the world, by men who have long since died and passed away. And, in the Hindu and Buddhist Scriptures they not only tell you what they have seen there but how you may learn for yourself to see and hear, which is a great advantage. And regarding it from that standpoint, I would say to you that things I am going to put to you as matters of my own experience are matters which you can evolve for yourselves if you will take the trouble, and go through the necessary study, but otherwise not. You cannot become expert in any science unless you give to it a great amount of time, sacrifice to it a great deal of leisure that might be employed in other things, and walk along the road laid down by others who have studied it, taking advantage of the methods which they have found to be satisfactory. Why then should you expect to do in occult science what you do not expect to do in any other science? If you want to be expert in mathematics, you cannot begin by using the results of the discoveries of leading mathematicians; you must study it for years; and not only must you study it for years, but you must also have brought into the world with you a special aptitude for mathematics, and that is a thing that people sometimes forget. I should say, as many people say nowadays, that this aptitude has come from study along that line in other lives; but however you think it came there you must recognise the fact that it is there in certain people, while others are exceptionally stupid over mathematics and may work at it all their lives without becoming great discoverers in mathematics or expert in the higher regions of the mathematical world. Now I may point out to you that these same conditions exist with regard to what I may call, in the general term, occult science—it means roughly certain knowledge of the laws of nature as touching the consciousness of man. And by utilising that knowledge and applying it specially to your own consciousness, shutting out things that would divert you from the particular methods you are following, you may then develop a condition of consciousness latent in everyone, but largely developed in those who are determined to become expert in the science in order that by its use they may become more helpful in the evolution of Humanity. I, therefore, am not making any excuse for saying to you things that you cannot at present verify for yourselves, except in a few cases. And you must judge for yourselves what amount of belief you think it reasonable to give.

There is one quality you must remember that is developed in many at the present time, which is developing fairly rapidly in very many, and is the special characteristic of that new sub-race to which I alluded, the quality that Bergson called Intuition. He defined it as an activity of the life, which did not look outwards, as does the intellect or the lower mind, but looks inward and by that development of life in the individual develops also certain organs, or will develop them he says, by which the quality may show itself as evolution proceeds. And he lays some stress on the fact that this new departure of human consciousness as he regards it is a quality rather allied to instinct than to the mind. The mind reasons from observations of outside objects; the instinct has been called accumulated experience—some would say accumulated experience of the race, others would say accumulated experience of that Inner Intelligence who is not mortal, who passes on from one body to another in successive life-periods, and who is that particular power in the human spirit who in the periods between lives upon earth has been in what many religions call the heavenly worlds, works up the experience of the previous life into capacities to be used in the next. Now, however you look upon instinct, you have there a case of accumulated experience, and it is that again carried on in the life which affects the body, the emotions, the mind of the people, of the animals who possess it. I have no time to dwell upon it in detail; I am only reminding you of that fact because it is an interesting fact to notice, that this is the quality which is appearing in this race, so that the young people possessing it do not find Truth by logical reasoning but by recognition of Truth by sight, if you will allow me to use that phrase. It is a remarkable change, and that is why Bergson does not look upon it as a development of the intellect, but rather that accumulated experience which shows itself by instinct in animals and man.

Supposing, then, you bring with you a great deal of that accumulated experience, you show it naturally in your thought, in your study, in your attempt to understand and analyse the world. You have that to a considerable extent, as you might have mathematical aptitude. You might not probably be able to develop in a single life that natural aptitude into a highly developed capacity of the illuminated soul of man. I will define "spirit" and "soul" in a moment. Looking at it in that way, I dare not say that no one of you can evolve it, but a good many of you ought to be able to do that, if you care to study.

Leaving that, then, aside, you might think I am merely dreaming or imagining. Let me look for a moment at this possible recognition of Truth at sight, for that has a very distinct bearing upon our subject. There are a large number of you who have not had experience of what I am going to deal with, but you may recognise, you may feel within you the recognition, that it is true, although you are unable to prove it, and that is a possibility open to a very, very large number. It is that quality to which the great Teachers have appealed when they have spoken of their own experiences, where they have dealt with the invisible worlds and helped in the building up of a new community on that basis.

Taking that, then, as a kind of general introduction to the rather unusual kind of lecture to which I proceed, I say frankly it is very largely personal, and that is not my habit: I generally deal with a subject, and knowledge gained by the ordinary study of the subject. This matter I must leave entirely to yourselves, but I remind you that the Scriptures were written by people who claimed to possess a great amount of that experience. I am not putting myself on a level with the writers of those Scriptures, but as having had experience which make to me credible other great experiences which are related in those great Scriptures of the world.

Now I do not know whether you have observed amongst different people a very different way of grasping Truth. Take an Irishman, take a German or English-man, and take one of this new type that is developing, and you will find a particular type of quality very different in those three people. In the Irishman, if you want to move a crowd, appeal to the emotions, hold up some great ideal, and your crowd will be fired by it. With the English-man or the German you must appeal much more to his reason, and convince that reason that the ideal is rational and useful. In the third case, you do not appeal either to emotion or to reasoning, but to that subtle quality I have mentioned, which we call intuition—and that principle to some extent is present in all of you, only it needs cultivation. Very many people when they get some idea, which they realise is given to them by the power of intuition, assume as they go back into their normal consciousness that it was imagination. Well, that is a very good way of killing the intuition, which is trying to bud forth from the seed which is latent in all of you. If you pull up a seed to see how it is growing, it will not grow very far, as we know from experience. Many people have found that, by always challenging their intuition and asking whether it was fancy or imagination, they have gradually killed out what I should call the intuition, and what they would call imagination. I only say that as a word of warning to those who may occasionally have glimpses of Truth, but are afraid to trust the God within them, who can only speak in a language which they are able to understand if He wants to influence them.

Now a Teacher has come on several occasions, as you know, in the Mother-race to which you all belong, and each time He has founded a religion. It is not then absolutely abnormal that there should be such a happening, and on the lines that I have traced in previous lectures you may very easily convince yourselves of the evidence for that. It has happened five times in the history of the great Āryan race. It happened for the latest time two thousand years ago, in Palestine, and there are evidences in the Gospel story by which the followers of that Great Being who, we should all agree, from the time of His baptism, when the Spirit of God, it is written, abode upon Him, was rightly called the Anointed, the Christ. Looking at that for a moment, there is a certain indication here and there in those experiences that the body He then took—as was asserted by a very large number of the wisest men in the Christian Church—was the body of a disciple named Jesus, and that that body which He used was used by Him for a brief period only, because His people murdered Him after three years of His presence—murdered His body I should say, after three years of His presence. And that section, the great Gnostic section of the Christian Church, always looked upon Jesus and the Christ as two separate Beings, of whom one of them, that great disciple, lent as it were the use of his body to the World-Teacher named the Christ, and that the Christ was the tenant of that body during the years of His ministry, although apparently with occasional interruptions, with which I need not deal. That then was the great theory of the past; it was denounced ultimately as heretic, and so dropped out of sight. I am going to put it to you that that was a true view. I am not going to say any longer "I believe," I am going to say "I know," because I am very often asked: "Why have you said certain things?" And it is a justifiable question. "Why do you think that the World-Teacher is coming?" "Why do you think that He is coming to use a particular body?" "What proof have you of such assertions" I say that I know that He is coming, and I will amplify that in a moment, because I have heard the Christ say so. I know that He is going to take this particular body, partly because I was told, while the body was that of a child, that he had been chosen for that special mission to the world, and the addendum was put, "If he grow up worthy for it, fit for it," and partly because certain things have happened which place that fact to me beyond dispute, not only in the invisible world but in the world down here. But I am going to say to you quite frankly I have no proof, what you call proof. A few of you have had the same experience, and the more people who have it the more credible will it be, just as when many people go to an unexplored country and they compare certain of the reports and find them agree. But if you ask me for proof that is convincing, I may answer, I am going to answer it, in two ways. First, that you have no proofs of those books which to you are most sacred, and the experiences of their writers: they are their own proofs, and that is the only proof that can come after the writers have passed away. Their effect upon the world, the change in human evolution that has resulted from them, those things may clearly be called proofs of some higher quality developed. We call it super-consciousness at present. And they are by the different religions of the world given special names. They are spoken of as prophets, sometimes spoken of as saints. But they were not as a rule justified in their own lifetime. As has often been pointed out, they were often put to death, and as the Christ Himself reminded the Jews, they built the sepulchres of those whom their forefathers had stoned. And that is generally the fate of those who come in a sense before their time in certain knowledge they have gained. That is a matter of small importance; its only value is that they have been justified by later facts. I may be justified by later facts, but that does not justify me now. Still, there have been many cases of such messengers sent to the world, and people have gradually found out by what they taught, or otherwise, that these messengers were true. I should say that the same proof could be urged in what I am going to say as was urged by the prophets at the time when they were told to carry a certain message, and had thrust into the human spirit a firm and deep and abiding conviction—which to those who have it is the one great proof of Truth and beyond all argument, beyond all intuition—when the Divine which lives in all of us, for our bodies we are told are the temples of God, when that Voice makes itself heard in the human spirit, then there is no longer possibility of doubt for the one who hears it, and he must take his chance in the outer world, even though he may be, as in the more brutal times, murdered or tortured, in more civilised times more gentle methods are used, and if he fears to meet these then he is unable to interpret that Divine Life. There are just four lines I have often quoted, because I think they put briefly and beautifully in the words of a poet that fact of experience which many believe in in others:

> Whoso hath felt the Spirit of the Highest
> Cannot confound nor doubt Him, nor deny:
> Yea, with one voice, O World, tho' thou deniest,
> Stand thou on that side, for on this am I.

And it may be worth your while to think over that, for the matter is one of supreme importance, to everyone of you, and to the world.

But now let me explain what I mean when I say I have heard the World-Teacher speak. All of you who believe in the Christ, and He is the World-Teacher of men of other faiths, who believe in Him though calling Him by different names—for when the prayers ascend to Him in India, they call Him Shrī Krishna—all of you who really believe and try to reach Him, can reach Him what is called subjectively; that is, in your meditations, or your prayers, or in any moment when your heart and devotion go out to Him, there comes to you an answer from the Invisible which you are likely not to deny. There is, I think, no faithful follower of the Christ who in some moment at least has not felt some response when he has called out to Him for help in danger, in sorrow, in difficulty. And that to millions of Christian people, and the same experience to millions of men and women of other faiths, who use other names but call to the same Great Being, these experiences are the deepest in their lives, and they would hold to them despite all denial from others. But the assertion of hearing seems to go further than that, for this is an objective word. And I assert that it is possible to reach that Presence of the Christ. Exactly how it is done you will understand when I come to the other lectures. Let me simply state it now as a fact.

Everyone of you has what I will put in the simplest form, in the words of S. Paul, a natural body and a spiritual body. Speaking a little more exactly, as to the human constitution, he divided it into three, body, soul, and spirit. The two words "soul" and "spirit" are very often spoken of as if they were identical, which is a mistake: S. Paul did not use words so carelessly as that. Thus you find each of these has its own characteristics, and in the body you include all that part of your consciousness which works through the brain and so on, that is the ordinary mind as well as the working of the senses. When you leave these behind, say when you are asleep, what becomes of them? The human brain is no longer recording them, the human senses are no longer affecting you with their observations, and the human mind, as far as you know, is asleep with you. But suppose these divisions are real, suppose you separate yourself every night when you go to sleep, leaving your body behind, your material body, your physical body, and the rest of you, with your consciousness, goes out in a subtler form of matter into subtler and invisible worlds? There again, when I come to deal with Western psychology, I shall have to go into proofs of that, but for the moment I leave it at that stage. The soul of man is the human intellect gathering up the thoughts and the emotions, the whole man so to speak, except his body and spirit, and most specifically the intellect itself. The spirit is the subtler form in which dwells the Life of God within us and the self-realisation of that Life.

Looking then at this division, is it so impossible that you might learn to keep your consciousness available when you come out of your body in sleep, and imprint upon your brain when you return the experiences through which you have gone in your subtler body, the body of the soul, as I will call it for the moment? There we will have a great deal of evidence from psychology when we come to deal with it in the West as well as in the East. Take it as a hypothesis for the moment. We assert that it is a fact, and that we have so trained ourselves that we have learned how to get it through, instead of going to sleep the consciousness remains intact, not in any way losing the sense centres with the lower world, but seeing and hearing and feeling and thinking and so on. Now the Christ is living in a physical body, very different from ours. Those of you who know your New Testament well will remember that He appeared to His disciples on several occasions after He had been put to death, and that that body had certain peculiarities: He could appear among them though the doors were all shut; he could disappear from them when breaking the bread in the presence of the two disciples at Emmaus. There are various cases cited in the Gospels and cited afterwards in some of the ancient books of His disciples. Clearly then the body that He was using then was not identical with the body He used upon earth while in the life of the body down here. That may give you some idea, not an accurate one, but sufficient for my purpose, of the difference between the body He is using now though living in a physical body in the Himālayas and that part of the body that he uses in His communications with His people all the world over when they address Him in prayer and meditation. The higher bodies of His are practically, some at least of His consciousness is, omnipresent, but in his physical, human body when He was here you find statements made by Him which show that for Him that was shut away from the human body. Those are indications that may make a little clearer what I am trying to convey, that it is possible by certain striving to learn to live in the higher consciousness, while the body is wrapt in sleep. In this condition you can travel very great distances, and you have knowledge how to go and whither: you may call it rather instinct than knowledge. I could not tell you in what part of the Himalayas He lives, because there are several parts of it from which the same view of the great plains is possible. He lives there in a very beautiful garden and looks over the plains of Northern India. A very large number of people are able to see Him there, and to hear Him. I happen to know a few people who have been with me in these travels in that land, and have heard Him say He is coming to His world. We had thought it would be later, but the world is in a state of crisis, which may have led Him to say the word that He was hastening His coming slightly.

Now that body which He uses in His secluded home is far too fine and too delicate to be subjected to the rough and tumble life down here: it would need an enormous amount of spiritual power, which could be better used, to use that body down here, and so, as on the previous occasion, He is utilising a body which has been carefully trained in purity of life for the purpose. Great purity is necessary, and great tenderness is necessary, and compassion for the sorrows of others. These last two are emotions, but they have a part to play in making that house of life fit for its Mighty Tenant. And that is one reason for a thing that may perhaps have seemed to you a little strange, the amount of seclusion and silence. Quite deliberately it was not talked about at the time, because otherwise it would have been impossible for the right training to be given. The time has now come when we are obliged to speak more plainly, and that for two reasons. First, that the way can be prepared by the testimony borne by a few, and by testimony borne to many. There is the great belief in all the great religions in the world, for all of them are looking to their own particular Founder, although they call Him by different names. That may be looked upon as accumulating evidence that some great event is coming upon the world, for the old proverb is true that "coming events cast their shadows before them". When you have Buddhists building temples, the Musalmāns quoting their own great Prophet that God would send a prophet to each new era, and Hindus looking for the return of Shrī Krishna, and a good many Christians looking for the return of the Christ, that widespread expectance is itself of much value, because it is so difficult to convince the whole world of the greatness of happenings in their very presence. Go back to old Palestine, when the Christ began His teaching there. Listen to the comments passed upon Him recorded in the Gospels: "How knoweth this man letters, having never learned?" when he read the Book of the Law and expounded its inner teaching. Notice the attitude of the Jews at the time, sometimes attracted in crowds, at other times angry, taking up stones to stone Him because He blasphemed, they said. Try and think yourself back into Palestine, as I have done very much in the last few years. I do not think the Hebrews of that time were so much to blame for their scepticism; but, if possible, it would be well to get a little of that over before He comes, again to be received with the same indifference, ridicule or scepticism, as the case may be. And that is why we are now talking quite plainly. That is why books are being written about these invisible worlds more plainly than ever before—other books about the great Masters, who are servants of the Christ, speaking of them, of their lives and of their disciples, in a way that we have never done, for the last year or two. For thus there seemed a chance at least that if it meant that some of the stones of contempt and hatred were thrown at us which otherwise might fall on Him, when He comes publicly out into the world, no longer as the disciple but as the Master of Masters, it would clear His path. That is one reason why I have been content that all kinds of things should be said, because if we can accustom people to the thought of these things beforehand, He may stay a longer time with us than He stayed with others in Palestine. He came then in the body of an oppressed race. The proud Romans, the Empire of Rome, looked down upon this Jewish Teacher with contempt. Is it strange if He should again use the body of an oppressed nation, and be despised by the European public who take part in that oppression? And so, looking back in that way, I have tried to make myself into a Jew of the time, and to understand how I should have looked at Him; and that has been a very great help to me. In your thought, can you try to think how they felt?

The people speak of what I said at Ommen last year. And quite naturally people say, "Who are you to be Apostles?" And they think it a position of great arrogance. But, after all, were the Apostles such very remarkable people in the days when the Christ was upon the earth in Palestine? Certainly not, if the story be true. Nobody knew much of them beforehand, until they went round the country with the Christ. And looking at them, were they worthy? I do not mean as to their rank. I mean as to the qualities they showed. One of them betrayed Him, one of them denied Him, and all of them forsook Him in the hour of His peril; and if that was the character of those who were with Him then, if you only see them through the dazzle of twenty centuries and hail them saints, try to put yourself back to the Palestine of the day, and say whether you would then have counted them worthy to surround the Great Teacher. No one is worthy of that; but at least some of us have been proved, that we have stood by the Truth when it was unpopular, that we have not denied the Truth we knew, that at least we may hope we will never be the cowards to forsake Him and flee in the moment of danger. But it is no great office remember, save in the spiritual world, the office of a close follower of the Christ. It is an office which, as long as the body holds it who has been given that work, has no honour. And if for the moment I speak only for myself, is there any reason why I should claim such a position except my belief in the Teacher, my knowledge that to serve Him is the greatest joy that life can give? But that is no proof. I do not pretend it is. I know myself as unworthy, far more than any others can know; for I know that one is less than the dust which is for Him to tread, as compared with the stupendous greatness of the Supporter, the Helper, the Guardian, of all the great religions of the world. But because it may make it a trifle easier for Him if one should speak out, I have spoken, and will speak again. I should not do it without the command of Those whose servant I am; but I hope I shall never be so base as not to obey Those whom I know as the great joy in life, who gave me the great joy of Divine Wisdom, and whom I can touch day by day in that life. And, friends, I would ask you to think that, after all, one does not say such words as I am saying, at my age and with my past, without giving at least some pledge of sincerity. For that I think I can claim. I have never been a great supporter of causes that brought honour and praise at the time. My path through life has been rather along other roads than those. I became a member of the Society when I was 42 years of age: I am now nearly 79, and to me the Theosophical Society is a thousand times truer and greater than I ever dreamed of it when I came into it in 1889. It has never changed to me. It has been an ever-increasing light. I joined it as the dawn, but now it is like the sun in mid-heaven. You do not want proof except the shining of the light, you know all you need to prove the sun when you walk in the light he gives. And is it not possible that in the twentieth century things should happen again that have happened so many times before? Is it so incredible a thing that He who loves the world and is its greatest Helper, that He should come again when the world is in the condition that it is in to-day? Is there any human wisdom that is able to solve the problems of the day? It would seem not. It is as though this country were in a tangle out of which it cannot emerge along the lines of its present system. If the Christ by coming to-day as He has done before, to lay the basis of a new civilisation, can solve matters, is not that a matter for you to think over yourselves, when you see two great warring systems one against the other— the system of social disorder and of struggle and a brotherly civilisation where man shall co-operate with man and not struggle as do the wild creatures in the jungle? Is it not possible that with His coming these great questions will find their solution? Is it not possible that the misery of our people through poverty, through suffering too great apparently for the ordinary State to grapple with, may find some help from Him whose wisdom "mightily and sweetly ordereth all things"?

Once through the mouth of His vehicle, on the 28th December last, He spoke for the first time in our lower world for some two thousand years. Krishnamurti was speaking, and it was evident that he was under very strong influence at the moment before he was taken possession of entirely, and I will read what he was saying, because it shows the influence that was then playing upon him. He had been speaking about the World-Teacher: "We are all expecting Him, Who is the Example, Who is the embodiment of nobility. He will be with us soon, He *is* with us now. He comes to lead us all to that perfection where there is eternal happiness; He comes to lead us, and He comes to those who have not understood, who have suffered, who are unhappy, who are unenlightened. He comes to those who want, who desire, who long—" The speaker started, stopped a moment, and then another voice rang out through his lips, a voice not heard on earth for two thousand years:

"I come to those who want sympathy, who want happiness;
   Who are longing to be released;
   Who are longing to find happiness in all things;
 I come to reform, and not to tear down:
   Not to destroy, but to build."

Those were the words that rang out above a crowd of some six thousand people. Some only saw a great light, some saw the Christ Himself, all heard the Voice. And that is one of the reasons why some of us are speaking so plainly about His coming, for that was to us, as it were, the birth of the Christ, His coming to the world, although only for a few moments, a reporter taking the words down at the time. And we watch and wait for that increasing Presence, by which the body will learn to bear the stress of that Mighty Tenant, becoming more and more susceptible until possessed wholly by the Christ, and only then will the World-Teacher be manifest therein, and those who recognise Him will find the help they want.

LECTURE II

FRIENDS:—

In speaking to you last Sunday you may remember that I said that up to that time, in lecturing on the coming of the World-Teacher, I had almost entirely confined myself to evidence drawn from history that could be examined by my hearers, so as to give them a ground for forming an opinion one way or the other. I also stated that in the lectures to be given now, I had taken another line of thought, but still one that is within the reach of the careful thinker, but, as I must admit, is not as readily grasped as the historical line; for when you come to deal with Psychology, it implies certainly an amount of study of the human constitution which is not at all necessary when you are dealing with the recurrent facts in human history. Necessarily, then, the proofs from Psychology will appeal to a smaller number of people, but still they are very, very important, if you want to understand even to a small extent the nature, the method, whereby the World-Teacher can come into our ordinary world, can come into contact with any one of us, can publicly teach, can lay down doctrines intended to form the basis of a new civilisation, and so, to the public of His own time, be a man among men. A very few moments of thought will, I think, convince you of that; and I shall say a word or two at the end as to what is meant by the consciousness of the World-Teacher. You must realise the enormous difference between that consciousness and our own.

Leaving that for the moment, the study carried on by psychology of the consciousness of the human being and its methods of manifestation in our world and in other worlds, must be confined either to those who study it carefully or to those who are sufficiently interested in a serious question as to gain a popular knowledge of the subject, sufficient to guide them in forming their opinions. I cannot hope to do very much more than that, and even then I am afraid that, specially to-night, you will find the subject complicated.

Now eastern psychology is very, very ancient. We cannot put a date at which it was not existent in our world; we go right back into the dark, and some of you may remember that a great German student of eastern literature said that the Vedas— part of the sacred literature of the Hindus—could not be put at a later date than 5000 B.C. Even taking that very modest measure of time we get back into a past where history, in the ordinary sense of the term, does not guide us; so we are thrown back on the literature of that country, which runs far beyond the 5000 years B.C., and which to some extent, by archaeological research, is being proved to be more and more dependable as a record of facts. I have no time to dwell upon that, but the 5,000 years, making, with the 2,000 of the Christian era, 7,000 from the present time, would do well enough as a length of time. I only want to remind you of its extreme antiquity.

Now, psychology from the modern standpoint is a very young science. I have specially said "modern" psychology, because the earlier psychology—save that of the schoolmen of the Middle Ages without going back still further to the great Roman and Greek writers—is very much on the eastern lines so far as the human constitution is concerned. I am concerned here rather with the very modern psychology, because it helps me in the object of these lectures to give you certain facts recognised by modern psychology which will enable you to grasp to some extent what is meant by a change of personality, that the human body may become separate from its ordinary tenant, and another tenant may step into it. That has been dealt with to a considerable extent in modern psychology, and that side of it seems to me worthy of study, especially in the West, where it is easily to be found, while the eastern psychology is not so easy to reach. It is true there is a great literature of translations, but even then the difficulty comes that unless the translator has some knowledge of the states of consciousness with which eastern psychology deals, it is very, very hard for him to translate by his own experience those states through which he has not passed. A certain grammar and dictionary knowledge is possible, but the knowledge of experience is lacking; and that is what makes translation of these ancient books so very unsatisfactory to those who have acquainted themselves, to some extent at least, with the language in which they are written; and then, by means of the practices that they recommend, have been able to experience the conditions which are described in these books.

And there is one fundamental difference between eastern and western psychology, not as regards psychology only, it is found also with regard to various sciences; the habit in the East was for the learned man to have practised Yoga to a very considerable extent; hence he was in the habit of beginning in the higher worlds and working down to the lower. Those conditions of human consciousness, which you have read of, at least, as being brought to you in the Mysteries of Egypt, of Greece, of Rome, of India, and so on, those conditions of consciousness were in the higher worlds; hence the student in the Mysteries naturally began with those higher and much simpler conditions, where unity had not become diversity as in the physical world to some extent; and from that he reasoned down from the inevitable results of his observations in the higher worlds and came finally to consciousness in such matter as we indeed at present find in the physical world. I have not time to dwell on that, but you may have noticed that alchemy came before chemistry, that astrology came before astronomy, and so on; the whole indication being that our modern sciences by observation of physical phenomena, beginning that is with these and working into the subtler regions of the physical world as now, that that is utterly different in its method from the eastern psychology and sciences, which begin on the higher and work down to the lower. I do not mean by that that when you begin the practical study you begin in the higher and work down to the lower; but I mean that you follow a certain series of experiments and experiences which you begin down here, following the instructions of your Teacher exactly on the same line that, if anyone is learning chemistry, he will be taught by a professor far more advanced than himself, and he will obediently follow the directions of that professor from the very moment he is allowed to handle anything which is dangerous from the chemical standpoint. No professor would take a pupil who refused to work for a time on the results obtained by those more advanced than himself; the professor would decline to risk teaching such a pupil, because it would be very easy to end in an explosion which would put an end to the researches of both the professor and the pupil. It is no enormous demand that if you are anxious to practise Yoga, you are bound to follow the person who teaches you, otherwise he will not teach you; and if you object to the conditions you must remain without the knowledge; just as if you wish to study chemicals and explosives you will not be allowed to have that knowledge, unless you follow the instructions given you, until you understand. It is not a case of blind obedience, which is to remain blind; it is a case of blind obedience of the ignorant to those who understand, in order that he also may learn to understand, and be able to walk safely along roads where ignorance means peril and may mean death.

Now looking for a moment, then, at that difference of method, you will be able, I think, very easily to recognise why it is that in eastern psychology you have exact descriptions of the higher and, normally to the ordinary man, invisible worlds, described with the same exactitude of knowledge which you would expect from an expert dealing with your own physical conditions. Clearly I cannot prove to you now that these are facts, because in order to prove them you must undergo the training similar to that through which I myself have passed. But I am not going outside to-night the general statements in books of psychology in the East, and those at least you can read for yourselves, and experiment to some extent, but not very far without considerable danger. And I ought, I think, to say here with regard to this, that there are a number of eastern books, known by the general name of Tantras (there is no translation of it, I mean the name, not the books), which deal with many forms of magic, and those have been to some extent translated, especially in America; these contain experiments which are exceedingly danger-ous, and it is a very common experience of my own in India that people who have tried these experiments without the conditions attached to their study under a Teacher, come and ask to be delivered from the results which have followed, primarily because they were not prepared for the studies they took up. You may say: "Then why were they published?" They were written in the language of the learned; they circulated amongst the learned, and always under the care of a Teacher. It is when they get published broadcast and anybody can take them up and begin experimenting along some of the lines, that one is bound to say: "These books are dangerous books." You can go through the earlier study; in the quite early stages the experiments there you can do simply by verbal instructions; but you come to what are called "magical processes," that means a knowledge of certain laws of nature, or a part-knowledge, by which you can bring about certain effects in this physical world, that you are dealing with forces like electricity, or higher forces of the same nature and even of a more powerful kind, and as they are controllable by the Will, there is very great danger in going into these practices unless you know how to guide yourself, and also unless your consciousness is sufficiently developed not to use them for purposes of personal gain, which leads to what is very often called "Black Magic".

Psychology in the East is part of what is very often spoken of as Philosophy. Philosophy is said to be that which alone can put an end to pain, and the object in all those systems in the East, the philosophical systems, that object is continually asserted as the one which is to be gained through Philosophy. You find such a simile, for instance, as: "Until a man can roll up the ether like leather, he will find no end to misery except by the knowledge of God." Looked at, then, in that way, you can very readily understand why it is said to put an end to pain. Brahman, the ordinary name for God (I shall use the word "God" as representing what is meant by the Samskrit word), is said to be "Bliss"; and when you go a stage further and find that consciousness is Divine, that there is only one Consciousness manifesting in different stages in the world according to its material vehicle; when you realise that the assertion that "God is Bliss" (and it is endorsed by every faith, I think), you will understand why only the knowledge of God can put an end to pain. Then the next step in philosophy—and here the branch of Philosophy called Psychology is entirely at one in the East and in the West—is that this One Consciousness exists as the Universal Consciousness, and also as the limited consciousness in the beings that live in this world. There are certain details given there as to the stages of the Divine Consciousness which show in the mineral, vegetable and animal kingdoms; and it is said that the whole of that in germ exists in the human spirit; that the gradual unfolding of it in the sub-human kingdoms leads on to the possibility of its much greater unfolding in the human spirit, and that therefore to man this knowledge of the identity of the human spirit and the Divine is supremely necessary. And in that way you come to what is called the "Great Sentence" of Eastern Philosophy and Psychology. It is contained in three words, but is known as the Great Sentence, and the three words are: "Thou art That." "Thou" is the human spirit. "That" the Universal Spirit; the difference not being in the fundamental nature, but in the unfoldment of the powers within. The human spirit is compared to a seed falling from a tree; all that the tree is can be developed in the seed, and nothing else can be developed in such a seed except the likeness of the parent tree. Looking at it, then, as a fundamental statement that "Thou art Divine" (I put the word "Divine" for "That"), you have the assertion that the human spirit, as it is called, is identical in its nature with the Divine Spirit; and on that Truth the whole of the great Philosophy of India in its highest form is built.

The greatest freedom of thought is encouraged on all these subjects. There is no limitation put to the power of the intellect; as far as a man can pierce the man has the right to go; for, naturally, believing that the Divine Spirit lives in every human being, he must come right in the end; no matter what his experiences are, they are only temporary; he can never be separated from the God within him; and the realisation of that God is the object of Philosophy, and the method of the realisation is found in the branch that is called Psychology.

Taking that, then, as a fundamental statement, we find that the Philosophy consists in everything that can be taught by one to another; and that is called the lower divine knowledge. The higher, the supreme divine knowledge, is the knowledge of God Himself, and that, it is said, can only be found by the man himself.

In order to aid his evolution, the science of Yoga has been laid down; so we can leave Philosophy on one side, the purely intellectual that can be taught, and turn to the other great branch, the scientific branch, in which the truths laid down by the intellect may be proved by certain definite psychological processes; and the further a man is able to follow out these practices, the higher will he penetrate into the mysteries of consciousness. Now the conditions laid down are quite definite. I said deliberately that there was no limit to thought, because one of the recognised systems of thought is often called atheistic; it begins with a duality, not with a unity; but Yoga is its complement; and sometimes you will hear Yoga called theistic Sāmkhya, while ordinary intellectual Sāmkhya is called atheistic; but it is not atheistic in the sense of denial; it only begins a stage lower down. I mention that because if you hear a thing called atheistic you may think freedom of thought has gone rather far.

In the practice of Yoga, first of all you must familiarise yourself with the constitution of man. Technical as it is, it is not difficult to grasp in its outline, and you will always remain in a condition of confusion unless you think it worth while to familiarise yourself personally with the outline at least of this philosophy, which enables you to understand the complexity of human nature, and to pass from one region to another of the invisible worlds. First of all, then, take that which you can prove for yourself, as quite a number of us have proved it by our own practice. Take it for a moment as a hypothesis, that our particular world—I confine myself to that—exists in seven conditions of matter—matter of different densities—and it is easy enough to make, as it were, a picture in your mind. If you think of that, then, the physical world that you know also consists of various densities and, according to eastern psychology, of seven densities of matter. First you have the dense physical matter, the thoroughly tangible and visible; your own bodies have that as part of their building up. Then, as you know, you have the liquid condition; also in your own bodies obviously. Then you have the gaseous condition, which is also in your bodies. Then you have what is called radiant matter, discovered here by Sir William Crookes only in our own time, what the East calls the lowest condition of the ether. Above that there are three other forms of ether, each with its own vibrations. Science recognises different vibrations in the ether. You will remember that Sir William Crookes made a very lengthy table and classified these vibrations, and these vibrations have been studied by western science. Eastern science gives the characteristics of each of them. Though all made of the same fundamental atom—I will use that word, without going into details—increasing aggregation characterises all these varieties, and that gives rise to some densities of the matter as we know by our consciousness; but we do not know these unless we have developed more than the ordinary sight of the eye, when the ether becomes an object of observation as well as gas. I am thinking of ordinary gases, as air; you can see the air vibrate where the sun is very, very hot. I have not seen it here—I have not looked for it—but I have in the East, about a hundred yards ahead on the road-surface when the sun is shining strongly. It is only a little extension of that, and then you will be able to see a good many things which you cannot see now. Still, take that as a statement of eastern psychology; this physical plane consists of matter of which the characteristics form seven different conditions, we call them sub-planes—"planes" is a very convenient word when you are dealing with a number of different densities of matter. As there are seven sub-planes here of physical matter, so there are seven planes in our whole world. I ought to say the physical plane is interpenetrated by these other planes, which extend beyond it on all sides as they become finer and finer; you have the intermediate plane, the world into which we pass at death; we call it the astral (a very unfortunate word); beyond that you have the heavenly plane of still finer conditions of matter, into which you pass after you leave your astral body, and there you remain, some of you, for what is sometimes a great period of time. As these different kinds of matter all enter into our bodies, the astral plane is better described as of emotional matter that is, the matter through which your emotions manifest themselves. The heavenly plane is better described as of mental matter, because that is the matter in which your thought becomes manifest. You probably know the Germans, who are very careful in their nomenclature, talk of "thought-stuff," "thought-matter." I do not know whether they talk of "emotion-stuff" or not, but I have come across the phrase "thought-stuff" in many of their books. So far, I have spoken of three planes, the matter of which enters into all your bodies, and you are constantly using the matter by which emotion shows itself and constantly using the matter in which thought shows itself. Now these three planes have nothing about them which ought to confuse you, because your own mortal body is working in all of them, only at different stages of consciousness. You have in the dense physical body what is called your waking consciousness which ought to be very much more extended, for you have also your emotional and your mental consciousness in that waking consciousness. The next stage has no English name; the best name, I think, is luminous consciousness. And then you have still the third state, spiritual consciousness. These, beyond the heavenly plane, are what is called "super-consciousness" in the East. Now eastern psychology says there are three mortal stages of consciousness, each of them having a plane of its own, reachable by human beings if they choose to take the method whereby they can penetrate into them. If you want to pass into the intermediate plane, then you would have— if you want to study it carefully—you would have at first to leave your physical body behind; so again if you want to pass into the heavenly plane you must leave your physical and your astral bodies behind you to go into that. And the whole of these three are mortal, having different periods of existence, the physical the shortest; then the astral plane with the astral body, though that may be a longer or a shorter one, according as the astral consciousness is used; the mental world may have a longer or a shorter life, according as your thoughts have been good or evil, going into high regions of thought or living in the lower regions, your stage in the heavenly world being entirely conditioned by those thoughts which you have had in your waking consciousness in the plane where all these three stages manifest. Your thought works through your physical brain. Your emotion works through your physical brain, and also, remember, through your nervous system very largely; thought again comes down to the brain through what is called the waking consciousness; consciousness in the sympathetic system is now sub-conscious, that is, it does not affect your waking consciousness. Now the latter part of that may be very largely understood and studied, as we shall see in the next lecture, but the way of liberating your waking consciousness and letting it pass into the other stages has to be gradually acquired. All these bodies are mortal; they are born into the plane, they belong to the plane, they die out of the plane they belong to, and the process of evolution is, of course, reincarnation. These are new every time; we call them sometimes the personality, that is to say, the mortal part of man. Then we pass beyond that. I have been dealing with what S. Paul calls the physical body. Then we pass to what is called the Soul, the individual, the ego. That to all intents and purposes is immortal. I have to say "to all intents and purposes," because at a high stage of evolution it merges itself in the Particular Spirit without losing its identity. Then beyond that ego, or individual, who has a plane of his own, the plane of the high intellectual, the abstract thought, of the lines of thought that do not deal with concrete observations but with abstract thought, which is applied to the observations in the discovery of, say, laws. Beyond that again the plane of the ego or individual according to eastern psychology, there are two remaining planes, the great plane of union, now beginning to unfold, where intuition has its place, and the last, the highest plane, known in the world as Nirvāna, should be familiar to all of you, but very much misrepresented, because it is thought of as though all were extinct, whereas the higher portion of man, the Spirit of man, uses all the functions he has gathered up through his evolution far better and more fully there than he could use them in the lower worlds. Now at first that may strike you as complicated, but it really is not, if you think it out. Seven interpenetrating planes, distinct by their atomic constitution in the ordinary sense of the word atom; each of these consisting of seven divisions, mortal beings confined to the first three, the practically immortal unfolded on the fourth upwards, and then beyond this the spiritual plane. There you have in a full form S. Paul's definition, he himself, of course, being an Eastern, of body, soul, and spirit. And that is really what you want to get a clear hold of, to realise that these are three distinct parts of your constitution, the three great states of consciousness recognised in the Eastern psychology. Then it goes on to say that each of these states of consciousness has its dwelling-place, its material dwelling-place. The third, the lowest, is the physical, the astral and heavenly, which are regarded as including all that is mortal in us, I speak so far as material is concerned, those three planes, the heavenly (or mental), the astral (or emotional), and the world of activity, these embody the waking consciousness of man. When we come to the world of the soul, his dwelling-place is in that higher condition of matter of which I spoke, and they called it the Radiant Body. It is the Augoeides of the Greeks, the ego, developed, immortal, but not eternal. You may remember that it is written: "God created man in the image of his own Eternity." That manifestation is everywhere recognised as triple, the Will, the highest manifestation, either in the Divine manifestation or the human of the Spirit; then Wisdom, which is Love illuminating knowledge; and then Activity, best described as the Creative Intelligence in man. In the ancient eastern faiths you always have this trinity represented as the One manifesting Himself in three qualities, Will, Wisdom, and Activity. It may make it perhaps more familiar if I use the Christian phrase, the Father, the Son, and the Holy Spirit. Will would be, of course, the Father. Then the Wisdom, which in Christianity would be called the Son, the Alone-born of the Father, and then the Creative Energy, the Holy Spirit. I am only giving you these three names that you may realise the meaning of that phrase, "God created man in His own Image", Will, man's highest quality. He gave also Wisdom, at a certain stage of his evolution; when Knowledge has been added to Love, that becomes Wisdom. Love is needed in order to turn the Knowledge into Wisdom. And then you have Knowledge the special property of the individual, the Intellect, which is said to be the greatest creative power in man. Remember the sentence, "Man is created by thought; therefore think upon God". The last four words are very often not quoted, because they may not fit in with the special argument, if it happens to be about the power of thought. But it is by thought that man creates himself in life after life, and that is the fundamental tenet of this eastern psychology. Pause for a moment on your waking consciousness. That is the consciousness which shows itself through your brain, but remember that in the eastern way of looking at it, that would be a very secondary division, because you would find any man with Yoga has practised the three first stages through which the consciousness of man passes. I do not want to worry you with Samskrit terms, because they are very minute. The ordinary consciousness of man is the one we are using at the present time; you are using your physical, your astral, and your mental body; they all work through your physical brain. You have the activity of the brain concentrated on a particular line of thought, you have the emotion, which may be stirred in the particular line of thought, and you have the mind concentrated upon that, the whole of these are impressed on your waking consciousness, and the accurate eastern psychology therefore calls these three bodies the dwelling-place of that particular state of consciousness. If you want to bring it down to the mere physical stages, we shall find that in the next lecture, and so I will only say for the moment that it is possible to separate your body made of the physical matter, it is possible to separate that from the emotional and the mental part; the emotional and mental part of the body goes out of the denser physical when you go to sleep, and there we shall see consciousness out of the body is spoken of as "dream consciousness". That is not the correct word to use, because it is not the consciousness of dreams really. Your body then, your physical body with its etheric part, you leave that every night in sleep. You ought not to leave in the etheric part of the body separated from the denser part; that gives rise to the phenomenon of mediumship. Mediumship consists in an abnormal condition, the physical dense body being apart from the etheric, and that etheric part oozes out from the spleen. It is visible for anyone who is slightly clairvoyant—it oozes out from the denser part, leaving only enough ether to keep the denser part together; that is really the danger in mediumship, because it lowers the vitality. The body, the dense body, and the etheric double ought never to be separated until you pass away at death, physical death being the separation of the etheric double from the dense body. Now in your ordinary normal sleep you leave your physical body and you go out in the rest of you, the emotional consciousness, mental consciousness with the ego and spirit. You may not yet realise the higher things of which I speak in your emotional consciousness; you very often get dreams, as they are called, and rightly so, but I would rather deal with them later. In your mental consciousness you come into a condition of your thought power which is far subtler and stronger than your ordinary thought. Any one of you could get experiences to prove that: if you put, say, a mathematical problem into your brain, as you would into a box, when you go to sleep, you must not work it there, you can get the solution as soon as you wake up. I used to do that when I was a materialist. It is a very simple test, demonstrating beyond question that you get into a stage of consciousness in sleep when the mind is more effective than when it is in the body, and that is an important thing. Anyone fairly well trained mentally can do it; I have done it many and many a time, when I did not believe in anything the other side of death. Artists get into that condition, emotionalists specially, as Mozart has told us, and so on. Think of that for the moment, because you will then get some idea of what is meant by a change in the personality. There is one difficulty I will deal with when we come to it. We may speak of a dual or multiple personality; and of the physical body as a house, the astral and mental bodies and the higher bodies working with them as the tenant. Suppose you do that deliberately, you would have to practise Yoga. But any of you who have lost, as you say, those who are gone from you by death, would be able to reach them if you thought of them just simply, quietly, lovingly, but without passionate grief, because grief makes the body vibrate so strongly that it drives away any approach. You may have sometimes a dream which is really a meeting with the one who has passed away on to the astral world. It is not so easy to reach them when they have passed into the heavenly world, until you have trained yourself to go there deliberately in full consciousness.

Now what are the conditions of learning this way of going in consciousness? You have three things to think of, the physical, the astral and the heavenly bodies, and you want to make your consciousness active in all these, so that when you return from the astral and the mental world you will be able to impress upon the brain the experience you have had there. That is the object. The first thing you have to consider is your physical body, and its nature, which is the great barrier in the way so far as you over here—I mean in the West—are concerned. You must have a pure body if you are to go out of it safely. I am not speaking of the sexual nature, though that is important, but you must feed the body on pure food; you must not eat meat, that increases animal passions, and you must not touch alcohol, because that works on a part of the brain which is used in this process later on; for if you meditate what is called prāna, Life, is sent to the pituitary body, and if that body is at the same time touched by the fumes of alcohol, through the inner nostrils, you cause inflammation, and enlargement of practically all the points of the body, the fingers, the toes, and the nose. Of course, the growth of the last one is a particular sign of taking too much alcohol, as anyone will tell you. You must face these things. You must not eat meat, partly because it is cruel, and you must be harmless so far as you possibly can, otherwise you go into danger. You must not touch alcohol. You must, if you want to do effective and good work, you must entirely leave off smoking tobacco. That is rather a difficulty, I am afraid, if I may judge from what I see, where some people cannot get through a meal without smoking between the courses. Well, I cannot change the conditions; they are not made by me. Some of you may say Madame Blavatsky smoked a great deal. In her latter days she did. She had done many "phenomena," and they had strained her body very much. She said to me once: "I give three years of my life for every phenomenon I perform." She did it for the purpose of serving the world. The result was she wrecked her nervous system, and as she had to keep the body alive for a certain time, she took to smoking to soothe her nerves. You will notice she did not work any phenomena in the latter part of her life.

These are the conditions which any Teacher would lay down if you wanted to learn the beginning of Yoga. Then you must practise harmlessness as far as you can possibly do it. I do not say you can do it entirely in this world of quarrelling, of wrong of all sorts; but you must aim at becoming yourself harmless, and that means great control over the emotions and the mind. Those, then, are the conditions as regards the physical body: great purity of life, in the fullest sense of the term. I have given you the three chief, as they may not have struck you; purity and then harmlessness, and then service to your fellow-creatures, because unless your social conscience is awakened, you would become a danger in the world into which you go. Then you have to deal with your emotions; you have to control these, and you can only control them by the exercise of the mind. There is a figure in eastern psychology that your body is like a chariot, the emotions are the horses, and the mind is the reins which the charioteer holds; and it is said unless you can pull in your galloping horses they will lead you into danger of every kind, and the only way to learn to control them is by meditation. Now meditation means concentration of the mind. That is the first stage. Then contemplation of that object of which you desire to gain knowledge; and then reaching up to that object of knowledge and identifying yourself with it, clinging as it were to that and absorbing its nature into yourself. First comes concentration, and you must learn that in order to control the emotions, and in using the power of concentration you must not have a thought of a weakness, of any fault that you may happen to have; thought is creative; if you think of a fault you strengthen that fault, you do not get rid of it; you must think of the opposite virtue; but all this you can read about in many books in English. These are the beginning of Yoga. They say some of my books are very clear; that is because I have practised. By practice along the lines I am speaking of you will have gained a very considerable power as regards the emotions, and by concentrating the mind on the astral world you will be able to develop your astral power and so become conscious in your astral body. But you have to turn attention outwards; instead of being concentrated on your own emotions, you must turn those emotions outwards and observe what is going on, and observe things which are going on as you do on the physical plane. All this takes a considerable amount of time. Most of you who have done any meditation will be conscious of a warm feeling in the body, down the spinal canal, sometimes like warm water running down. That is one of the signs of meditation, that you are beginning to affect certain sleeping forces within you. You hear a good deal of Kundalini. All that I can say about that is that it is one of the dangers in meditation. This lies in the nature of the etheric power, which is like a fire: it is the fire of creation. That fire may be used normally between husband and wife when a child is to be born, but the other deliberate use of it means that you gain such control over it that you can move it by the force of your thought and will, and then you send it upwards, upwards to the brain, where that creative power is lodged. You pass it on the way through seven different points in your body, through what are called chakras, and that is the thing which no one will tell you how to do, unless you are living a purely celibate life, because the danger of this creative fire is very, very great. Now these chakras are certain points in the body, and it may interest you to know I saw a remark in the newspaper that a number of people in the south who were studying under Krishnamurti made the sign of the Cross, that they were going to make it in Hindu temples, and that was going to cause rioting. Evidently the writer did not know that long before the Christian era the sign of the Cross was made in India, and for the same reason. It is a very ancient sign. The Hindus have always used it, and use it to-day. There is a very slight difference between the Hindu and the Christian in making the sign: the Hindu touches the top of the head, which is the passage by which the subtle bodies leave the physical body; that passage is open. And on the top of the head is a point just where you see a pulse beat in a baby, (as you get older it is covered by bone), there is a place which is not quite closed. The Christian touches the forehead, because it has the same effect. The Hindu touches the heart also, and then back to the right. The same sign, and the same effect, stirring the higher centres into activity, those that are above, as it were, the waistline and are used by the higher powers. And that is the reason why the sign of the Cross is used. I do not know whether very many Christians who are not instructed in occultism know the fact, but the Hindus find it in their books. They very often use a. little water at the same time—sacred water. That is a perfectly safe sign to use, and wisely used when concentrated thought after a time carries the person immersed in meditation out of their body with full consciousness. There is no danger in it, provided your meditation is on a high subject, some object that you revere; it may be the Christ, it may be a great saint, one of the angelic host, something that is far above you, and then the sign of the Cross is helpful, and if your meditation be strong and your thoughts disciplined you would pass out of your body consciously into the intermediate and higher worlds. Now that will enable you to realise how a change of personality may take place. But suppose you ask me: "When the World-Teacher occupies the body that He has chosen as a physical vehicle, what will be the effect of such possession?" I must ask you for a moment to try to imagine—we cannot, none of us, really dream—what the consciousness of the World-Teacher is; remember He hears every prayer addressed to Him, from every faith, from every longing and devoted heart; His consciousness is omnipresent, not only for our world but other worlds as well: that consciousness responds, the people of every religion can bear testimony to that. And if you ask me how such a Consciousness can occupy a physical body, and what will be its conditions when thus occupied, my answer is: "I do not know." Who am I, who is anyone, to say what that Consciousness can do and what it cannot? Certainly, as I have told you, I have seen the physical body worn in the Himālayas, but that is a very different body from the body worn down here by ordinary people: that body responds to every touch of consciousness, but even then the consciousness exists where that physical body cannot follow it. I have no idea, therefore, how that Consciousness, or how much of it, if one can use that word reverently, can inhabit the limitation of the body of the physical man.

There is one phrase: "I established this Universe with one fragment of Myself, and I remain." Shrī Krishna spoke, and he is the same as the Christ. How are you and I to judge, how can we judge anything but foolishly, of such omnipresent Consciousness? And so I prefer to say quite frankly: "I do not know." What I do know is that it would be worth while to learn from the study of the Christ when He is passing through before us. I hope I shall be wiser than I am now ten years hence, but I cannot tell you any more than I can tell myself. All I can say is that some fragment of the Mighty Consciousness will take up its abode in a body chosen, out of which has passed for the time all the consciousness normally present in it, leaving only the physical consciousness, which is sub-conscious, remaining. That is one way in which it may be taken possession of, but there are many other possibilities. The one that we know as Krishnamurti will step out, as he (Krishnamurti) does every night in his sleep, and I presume will remain ready— being the whole consciousness except the physical expression of it—and the fragment of the Great Consciousness will occupy that physical body. That much, at least, we know, because we have heard His voice through it. I imagine, but this is only my imagination, that such a manifestation will take place more and more continuously as the body becomes able to face the enormous strain, because we know that the strain is terrible even for a moment or two of such inhabitation. And that is why he remains so very much in quiet seclusion. Clearly the body has to become accustomed to its great work. I cannot tell you how long that is going to take. That body is exquisitely made for its work in every way: it has been kept and guarded so that it should remain as pure as a human body can be kept in this world, so that the Mighty One can take possession of it as His vehicle. So if you can think of that consciousness, that omni-consciousness of the Christ, you will realise why it is I have tried to get rid of the idea that my much-loved son and late ward—Krishnaji we call him—is the Messiah. That is a word I never use, because it is a local word, and would not be understood in other parts of the world. To me it is blasphemy, and to him it is blasphemy, to speak of him as the World-Teacher. And if you have been able to follow me in a very difficult subject to-night, I think you will be able to realise a little of the possibilities of such occupation of a physical body, and to realise the enormous difference, even when the influence is very, very strong; and you will understand that none of us who know a little about it would ever say anything so blasphemous as to say that he is the World-Teacher. We know a little of what the World-Teacher is, but how little! and certainly it is our duty to protest that no mortal human being should be identified with Him, save as he is taken temporarily as a vehicle through whom that Teacher may touch the mind and consciousness of man.

LECTURE III

FRIENDS:——

I shall have to ask you, in accompanying me over the ground which I have to traverse this evening, to remember that very much of what I say, for thorough understanding, will require study on your own individual part. Just as in the case of last week I had to deal with a very complicated subject in the ancient or eastern philosophy and psychology, so again to-night, although not so complicated in detail, we have to consider many concepts which are somewhat foreign to the more modern mind of our time, which deal with observations made by the senses and studied by the mind in order to base conclusions upon them, rather than with that method both of the older and of the comparatively modern psychology, which is studied by the intellect first, by strenuous efforts of hard thinking. So you are face to face with a study which is the work of men of the highest intellectual power, who faced the great problems of existence. Then you have also to consider the very modern psychology which is experimental in its nature, which tries to climb up from observations made on the consciousness of people in the physical body and by collecting enormous numbers of remarkable cases to build up in that scientific fashion a theory which will explain them and, as it ought to do, unify them all—that search after laws along the ways of modern science, which after innumerable experiments tries then by an intellectual effort to find out the law which underlies those varied experiments. Now psychology has one peculiarity in regard to these two kinds of investigation. The earlier one is separated from the later by a great gulf of scientific materialism, which breaks as it were into the current of human thought and separates the older modern from the very modern; and we are bound, I think, in making allowance for that, to remember that the conflict between religion and science was so bitter before science had gained strength enough to defend itself, that those of us, who regard the explanation connected with religious philosophy as the more satisfactory, are bound to admit that the provocation came from religion and that the antagonism of modern science—it is now growing out of it—which characterised it in the last century was very largely a reaction against terrible persecution, and was an effort to establish the right to think on whatever subject was cognisable by the human mind. Modern psychology is in the experimental stage, is very young, it must be remembered, in the West. Except along a comparatively narrow and very difficult path followed by a few, it had not the advantage of that science of Yoga which we have seen accompanied philosophic investigation in the East. Thus very much was lost, for with the absence of experimental verification the philosophical concepts came to be out of relation to life. That same difficulty is found at the present time in India with the great pandits whose philosophy is magnificent, but very largely, with many of them, only a matter of commenting on the past and not of verifying in the present. Yoga in India has largely been overlaid by modern scepticism, and that has deprived the eastern psychology of the very widely spread evidence that once accompanied it, and which is still more or less regarded as necessary to high spiritual attainment.

Now, when we think of the philosophy which gave birth to psychology in the Middle Ages—very modern, remember, in the history of thought—inevitably we shall find, as we study, much eastern thought; because in the higher regions of the intellect certain phenomena are necessarily observed in consciousness, which are the same with all who reach the higher regions. This is more remarkably true when you come to deal with Mysticism in the West and with the science of Yoga in the East, because the mystics have similar experiences, and the testimony of consciousness in East and West is the same practically as regards those who, by devotion, by what is called sometimes ecstasy, come into direct touch with the higher worlds and also into direct communication with the Divine Spirit.

Now there is one name that stands out in this modern philosophy and psychology, we may say above all others, I think, in its results upon the world of thought in the West. That name, of course, is one familiar to all of you, in name at least—that of S. Thomas Aquinas. He is very often called the "Angelic Doctor," and I have sometimes been puzzled as to why that particular name was given to him. I am inclined to think that it was his wonderful profundity of thought, his extraordinary courage in facing the most difficult problems of existence, which made many who reverenced him, but could not emulate his work, regard him as though he were illuminated with the angelic, the spiritual type of intellect, which contains all knowledge, while the human intellect acquires it stage by stage. Whether that be only a fancy or not I cannot say; but the name is very commonly given to him, and his immense importance now is that his so-called speculations, which were really the result of the highest philosophic intellect, give us a very much clearer and more definite idea of the laws underlying the modern experimental discoveries than, as it seems to me, is given by those who are making and studying with what Clifford once called the "sublime patience of the investigator" this very obscure region which they are trying to pierce by means of experiment in the physical world. Looking at that, it is only fair that we should remember that this science is very young, that the experiments which have been made, wonderful as they are, hardly perhaps give a basis for a really satisfactory explanation; for, as I shall have to put to you in connection with these, they start with a somewhat surprising theory of the disintegration of the personality. The personality, you must remember, looked at from the standard of consciousness, is regarded quite rightly as triple: the sub-conscious, the conscious, and the super-conscious—perfectly fair and right divisions are these of states of consciousness, but, when too much stress is laid on the sub-conscious, it leads, I think, to confusion of thought. There you must each of you form your opinions for yourselves and, according to the special line of your studies, you will reach thereby one or other of certain definite conclusions.

Let us then, for a moment, try to grasp the bases of the great philosophy, of which, as I say, the best exponent is the "Angelic Doctor," its importance to us being not only its profound interest as a triumph of intellectual genius, but also for the very practical reason that the whole of the teachings regarding the constitution of man in the great Roman Catholic Church are judged as to their orthodoxy by the measure in which they reflect the philosophy of S. Thomas Aquinas. It therefore inevitably has a very strong influence on that great branch of human thought among the enormous number of believers in the Roman Catholic Church, and we have to remember, therefore, that the modern writings of psychology of the learned of that Church will practically be a kind of summary of the teachings of S. Thomas, difficult perhaps to follow, unless one has at least some acquaintance with the writings of the Angelic Doctor himself. I am obliged in dealing with him, for lack of time, to make assertions about his teaching rather than give a number of quotations. I am not putting them, of course, as my own opinions, much as I have learned from him, but I am putting them distinctly as his teaching on certain profound subjects dealing with the constitution of man. He accepts the normal definition of that constitution as triple: body, soul, spirit. With that we are all familiar, although we have very little idea, for the most part, as to the difference between soul and spirit, and one great merit of the psychology of S. Thomas is his exceedingly luminous concept as to the nature of the soul. It is very subtle and is worked out with extraordinary acuteness of intellect. How far, at the moment, you will find it helpful or, as I called it, luminous, will a little depend on how much of this conception has already entered into your own studies so that you realise its far-reaching character; and I think I may venture to say it is unique in character in this modern philosophy and psychology—unique, that is of course, in the West. He lays down first as an ultimate pair of incompatible existences: spirit on the one side, matter on the other. Those two form the first pair of opposites in Hindu philosophy, as very many of you may know. They are, so to speak, although this is not S. Thomas's idea, complementary to each other: what one is not, the other is. But he takes them as entirely antagonistic; incompatible with each other is the idea on which he lays stress; so that spirit is absolutely apart from, not necessarily antagonistic to, matter; it is a later and less intellectual conception that spirit has nothing in common with matter. There you have a primary basis for his philosophy. He then goes on to define what he means by spirit, and he tells us that there are many grades of spirits, that they are alike in their qualities although not in the extent of those qualities. The highest of all he says is the Universal Spirit—God. All beneath that may be classed as Particular Spirits, that is, spirits who, if we could use the word without trenching on his thought, we might call individual, and he points to many orders of the angels, to many types of human beings. Also to those who are spoken of as fallen angels, or more ordinarily now as demons or devils; all of these, he says, after the soul has come into touch with the human being, are grades of spiritual beings and the lowest of these is the soul. Think then simply of that great ladder, a kind of Jacob's ladder if you like to have that, with ascending and descending spirits. All of these have certain qualities in common, and these you must accept for the time if you would follow his line of argument. First of all, he says, having nothing in common with matter, they are not subject to the laws of space and of time, the two great conditions, as you know, of human thinking. Space for them, he says, is non-existent; they are where they think. Now, as that idea for a moment may seem to you altogether impossible, let me just remind you in passing that we find, on examining consciousness, that the finer and finer the matter is in which it is working, the more tremendously rapid are its movements, and that is not only characteristic of thought, but of certain subtle forms of vibrations in the ether. Think for a moment of the speed with which electricity travels; yet you know that thought can travel faster than electricity. Take any case you like of subtler and subtler matter, and you are beginning to realise that electricity of a kind can travel without the assistance of the material wire along which we used to send our telegrams. Carry that further and further in thought, and compare with that the sluggish movements of physical matter, and you will see that it is only going a little further, as it were, when you are dealing with the spirit, to realise that the movement of that—he would not say movement, I am putting that in to make it much clearer—may be so incredibly rapid that it may be inappreciable; that the very thought may be so swift that the spirit, unencumbered by matter, is where he thinks.

Then again, time: time is measured here by material bodies and certain movements. Duration, he says, there is. But the difference between time and duration is that time is as it were fixed by the movement of certain bodies, by which we calculate. Duration is measured by intensity of thought.

There again, modern science may help you, for in a study to which I must draw your attention presently—the study of dreams—it has been found that dream time, or duration rather, is extraordinarily different from earthly time, although apparently it is going on in connection with the same brain. I shall have to come back to that to give you just one or two instances to show you how it works; but there again you can imagine that, in connection with finer and finer matter, thoughts increase in rapidity of succession, so that many ideas which would take comparatively long in the physical brain would flash faster and faster as the matter they are sheathed in becomes finer.

Then again, you will find that, by throwing out your thought a little further, it is not so impossible to realise that which he always declares, that time is an illusion. We are bound by it here so long as we are only using physical consciousness, but we are forced into the realisation that thought is not limited by time, as are the actions to which it gives birth in the physical body.

Those two conceptions, then, of the angelic existence are not, if you think them out, so very impossible to conceive; anyhow, that is the view that S. Thomas takes. In dealing with that you may go just one step further in regard to the nature of intellect, as he says it exists in the spirit, to intellect as it exists in man, for there we come into the domain of the soul. You must have had in your thought, as I have been speaking, the idea that if spirit and body, which is matter, are so entirely incompatible with each other, how is it they are brought apparently so nearly together in our physical world, what can be the connection between these two incompatible existences? S. Thomas's answer is: the soul. Now the soul, you may remember, was the lowest type of the spiritual gradations. The universal is the highest; the particular is the intermediate, and then the soul which has some characteristics which make it certainly still a spirit, but something has entered into its being, which enables it to influence matter, and there arises a conception that many find it difficult to get hold of. It used to be called at one time substance: that is the idea which makes a particular material object the material object which it is. Take wood, ordinary wood; wood may differ very much in its ordinary constitution and everything else, but there is something, the idea of what the workman is going to create out of the wood which makes him give to that wood a particular shape and utility, which makes it an article, an article of use to ordinary people. Now that is a concept very constantly found in the Middle Ages, though rather objected to in modern times. But you will find in all the great religions the idea that thought precedes creation of objects. The Jews will tell you in their famous Kabala that the world of ideas precedes the world of form or things; and that, when you come to think it out, is absolutely true all round, because no one can make out of ordinary matter an article which is to be useful and serve a definite purpose, unless he has an idea in his mind as to what he is going to do with that matter. You know it perfectly well, put in that way. It is according to the conception of that worker that the matter takes on particular forms and utilities.

There is nothing recondite in that; it is round us at all times. Now when the philosopher was considering that thought precedes form, he necessarily put it in an abstract and general way. All the worlds are God's thoughts, you will find sometimes stated, and the power of thought in man, we are told in Scriptures, is creative, creates an act, and is more important than the act itself. "Man is created by thought," we may quote from the East, I quoted it the other day. Take the words of Christ: "Whosoever looketh after a woman, to lust after her, hath committed adultery with her already in his heart." Always the thought before the outer manifestation. Now the subtle metaphysical and philosophical thinker is not content to put it in that very general way, but works it out, and so S. Thomas put it very strongly, and others followed him, that the soul was the agent who stimulated thought, elevating the senses which supplied to the intellect the material on which it formulated ideas; the soul was a spiritual substance that gave form to matter, that which made it what it was in the material world, the form in which that idea could be expressed. Then you come to the further refinement, which is only wanted in argument really, that while the real substance is the idea, the outer matter in which it embodies itself is the accident, or accidents, in which it works. Any outer body depends on the thought behind it. Then, if you can change the thought you may perhaps not change the outer appearance, for matter is very resistant—one of its qualities being inertia—but you change the essential nature of the thing, leaving unchanged its clothes of matter, and that is the essential idea of the soul. The soul comes into touch with a human body. A human body without soul, said S. Thomas, is the body of an animal; if you could conceive a man without soul, he would be simply an animal: he has animal passions, many animal organs, and the whole body is under the ordinary physical laws of growth, of evolution also, for you must not quite forget that the idea of evolution did not begin with Darwin and Wallace; you will find, for instance, in the writings of one of the metaphysicians, Mesnavi, in the Middle Ages: "I died out of the stone and I became a plant; I died out of a plant and I became an animal; and I died out of an animal and I became a man: when did I ever grow less by dying?" It is a very fine thought. And so, taking that view, the outer form of man—derived from the animal kingdom, subject to the laws of animal life, living as regards his passions, his appetites, his impulses, his organisation in a body like that of the animals—becomes with the touch of the soul a rational being. Those are the words by which S. Thomas distinguishes the function of the soul, and this is the advantage of the soul being as it were brought into touch with the body that, having the material of all these living passions to work upon, his function is to raise them to a higher point. As an illustration, the mere craving of the animal after its mate, the mere physical sexual craving, becomes in the man the splendid sentiment of love. It is raised from the lower to the higher, and an emotion is the touching of passion by thought, a mingling of thought with animal craving, for thought remembers and thought anticipates, and the remembrance of the love that brought together husband and wife would endure through times of her sickness, her weakness, and so would become touched with that splendour of endurance which raises human love into the likeness of the divine; that is the great function of the soul. Take all the lower feelings and senses and raise them; and then it becomes possible that the soul, on its spiritual side, can come into contact with, be one with, the spirit; it is a spiritual being endowed with this formative power—for that is what it really is—who becomes the link between

27

spirit and matter and makes man what he is. S. Thomas, of course, says—I ought to say that in passing, perhaps—that he regards the animals as having souls, but not as having souls that are spirits. I do not know why he makes that distinction, but he does; he says that all spirits are not souls, and all souls are not spirits; so that he does not regard the animals as having the possibility of the life of the spirit, or of receiving a like stimulus from the nonhuman soul.

Taking, then, that concept as it is, whether you agree with it or not, we have to regard intellect as the great characteristic of the spirit, and human intellect is limited to that which through the body you can observe. There you come to a very important distinction: it is an axiom of the Roman Catholic theology, derived from S. Thomas that there is nothing in the intellect which is not derived through the senses. Spirit has all knowledge in it of its own innate nature, if I may double the expression. Knowledge belongs to the spirit, complete in itself. And there again is a curious touch with the Hindu thought, which, dealing with the ego, the higher intellect, says that "his nature is knowledge". Hence you have philosophy as Leibnitz defines it in his definition of knowledge. When he speaks of perfect knowledge you may remember he says it is intuitive, and that is very significant as regards the way in which knowledge is recognised. In the lower mind you argue and gain your knowledge from observation and logical argument. In the higher kind you recognise truth—I am taking one case—at sight, because his nature is knowledge; all that is not true causes a jar. It is that direct perception which the musician has of a false note in music. He does not argue about the vibrations that go to make up a dissonance that strikes his ear. He says the note is sharp, is flat, it is false. Similarly the higher intellect, the spiritual intellect, whether in man or in angel, knows truth at sight by that same instinctive recognition the causing of a jar in himself unless it is in accord with his own nature. And those definitions are very useful for accurate thinking, although they may be a little tiresome when you come to deal with them merely as matters of study and not as matters which can be experienced. That point I shall want to deal with next week, because I shall not be able to deal with it at present; I may just remind you that you would be thinking unfairly if you took it that the philosophy of the Middle Ages had not the central idea of Yoga, although that is one of the points I must deal with next week. You do have a very definite science of Yoga in connection with certain training of consciousness and the only difference you may see between that and the very ancient psychology of the East is that while the Eastern would say a spirit in man, a Particular Spirit, gains union with God, the Western Yoga says that man reaches deification. That is the Roman Catholic phrase from a very remarkable book called *Interior Prayer,* but it does not seem very much to matter whether you say that man is united to God or whether you say that man is deified; the idea is the same of a perfect union of spirit.

I must now turn to the experimental view, and I may put to you, not thoroughly fairly perhaps, the thought that is in the mind of those who have made some most remarkable experiments which are very useful to us all, who believe in the possibility of more than one personality inhabiting one body. It seems to me confused, though I may there do it an injustice, but the idea is going back to the sub-conscious and the conscious. The personality includes a third: the super-conscious. The sub-conscious is given enormous importance. It is, as it were, the reservoir of the past and that reservoir of past experience is below what is called the threshold of consciousness, but sometimes it bursts over that threshold and then you get tremendous surges which dominate the waking consciousness and force it along a line that otherwise it would not take. Out of this idea of the sub-conscious there grows up the further idea that the personality is a very complex thing, consisting, as far as I understand, of many groups of experience, many of which have fallen into the sub-conscious, and are therefore not in the waking consciousness. Those groups, it is contended, may and do appear in the ordinary person thrown out of gear, as it were, by some mental or physical disturbance, so that the group which is not normally present may surge up from the sub-conscious and overcome the ordinary waking consciousness, and that gives rise to the phenomena of a dual personality or a multiple personality, or other special phenomena which occur, and have been very carefully observed. Now I said that this very modern psychology began with the study of the dream state, if you remember. Let me give you one illustration, because it has gone far, far beyond the study of the ordinary dream. You can find any number of illustrations in Du Prel's Mysticism. I am taking one remarkable case from it; I think there are hundreds of cases given. The experiments, made to find out what a person thought while he was dreaming, were carried out by suggesting a dream and suggesting it by a touch on the external body. The one I am thinking of is this: they touched the back of a man's neck with a sharp knife, just enough to make a pressure of the sharp edge, but not enough to injure; it woke the man. During that brief space of time he had had a very long dream. He dreamed that he had murdered a man, that he was arrested, that he was tried—and he went through the whole of the trial—that he was found guilty, was condemned to death, was placed in the condemned cell and then was guillotined. Now, of course, in many cases that result would not be gained. They tried a huge number of cases, and there is no doubt that you can so impress a body with a momentary contact that that body may carry out a long succession of events. There is a great difference between an imaginative person in that, and a person of dull and uneducated thought. That came out in an experiment of sprinkling water on the face of two people, one of whom was an ordinary country peasant and the other a man of great intellectual power. The water was sprinkled at the same moment. It woke each of them. The one man had only dreamed of a thunderstorm: that was the peasant. The poet saw a splendid landscape, under a thunder-storm with flashing lightning and rolling thunder, and he drew an elaborate verbal picture of that when he woke up. Both had been asleep at one time. That naturally gave rise to a further investigation to try to catch the dreamer, because he was not of much use if he woke up at the very moment when he was most interesting, and they found a way of catching the dreamer, and that was by throwing him into a trance.

Now a trance might be brought about by mesmerism or hypnotism, and the most careful observations in some ways have been made by the latter, on more or less hysterical patients in the hospitals for hysteria in France and elsewhere; others have been made more satisfactorily by mesmerism in which you take the normal person, throw him into a trance, so that his body is insensitive, but so that you can make him see or not see, according as you desire that he should see or not see. In the first cases of experiment generally the thing was done by throwing a person into a mesmeric trance and telling him to go somewhere and tell you what he found. I can give you an illustration of Charles Bradlaugh, who had very great mesmeric force. He was a materialist. He had very powerful mesmeric force and he used very often to mesmerise his wife; he was very interested in it, and tried to find out how the action took place, and one day he sent her in a trance to his printing office and asked her what she saw there. She said: "Oh! the stupid woman; she has put in a letter upside down." What the letter was I do not know, but I had the story from Mr. Bradlaugh himself. Then the next day the proofs came. Naturally he turned to the proofs, and he found that the printer, the compositor, had put in the particular letter she had noticed in a word, upside down. That is what she had observed. I think they were in Leeds at the time, and that was going on at the London printing office. That is a very common illustration, but you may find any number of such in the different books. When you come to more careful investigation than that casual kind of experiment, you may follow the dreamer in the trance, the body being entirely insensitive, only to be waked up by the person who has thrown it into that trance. At one time I did a great many experiments when I was studying psychology, because I was very puzzled by the materialistic explanation of it which did not explain anything. In those cases you can make a person see what you want him to see; make him hear what you want him to hear; and he will not respond to anything else. You may make him see a blank paper on which he will draw pictures projected by your thought. You may make him hear a sound; he will tell you what it is, and so on. All those are preliminary experiments, and they all lead up to that experimental psychology in which very remarkable results have been found. That is the origin of a very large book you may have seen, Myers' *Human Personality.* I have picked out four special cases because they illustrate four different types of change of personality. The first of them is a case in which there was projection of the personality of the living person separated from the body that he was normally wearing. That first experiment I give you since it is peculiarly illuminative, because you will find that you had three witnesses: two ladies who were together in the room where it took place and, some years afterwards, the person who had projected his own form into that room. I am taking this very projection of personality from the well-known book of Myers, and he himself took it from the book of his friend Gurney. (The name of that book is *The Phantasms of the Living,* where you can find an enormous amount of information on this particular point.) The names of the ladies, who were together, are given. It was an elder lady travelling with a younger one and taking care of her and travelling to Egypt. There was a great crowd and they had to go to a very unfrequented hotel. They were rather nervous, and they were shown up into a room on the third storey which was very desolate and gloomy, and the young girl especially was frightened. The elder woman took precautions against anybody coming into the room, and she gives the first account of it. This Mrs. Elgee, as her name was, said she locked the door, and as there was a very heavy settee in the room, the two of them dragged it across, leaving it so that it had its weight against the door. To make that further secure, she put her travelling bag on the settee so that it would tumble down and wake her up if anybody tried to come in through the door. She remained awake, and she tells what she saw: how she saw a friend of hers—whom she had left behind in England, and with whom they were very intimate, and who had often referred questions of difficulty to her—she saw him in the room. She says that she saw him so clearly by the light of the early dawn coming in through the large window. "He appeared eager to speak to me, and I addressed him with, 'Good gracious! how did you come here?' So clear was the figure that I noted every detail of his dress, even the three onyx shirt-studs which he was wearing." Then he came a little nearer to her, she says, and looking back she saw her friend shake his head at the figure of Miss D.—that was the girl—who was sitting up in bed gazing at the figure with an expression of horror, and so the figure retreated and disappeared. Then the elder woman asked the girl what she was looking at and what had frightened her, and she said: "There is a man in the room." The elder woman would not tell her she had seen it, but laughed at her, and said: "It is only your fancy; you are afraid." The girl said it was not her fancy, and she described the figure, she gave a description of this particular person. A long time afterwards the third person comes into it: the man who came there. And the elder lady says: "I fear it is quite impossible to get any information from Miss D. She left afterwards, and my visitant also is dead." However, later on she met Miss D., who had then married, and she told her that she was travelling in India, going to rejoin her parents, she was going out to marry her then husband, Major So-and-so; she gives an account of the whole thing, and finally she mentions that this visitant, the living man, had left behind him a statement that he was sitting in his room one night at the time, the month in the year, that Mrs. E. had seen him, with a most intense yearning for her advice and assistance. So great was it, that he felt as if the invisible power had drawn him into some spirit state in which he could and did see her. Well, that is not the only case I can give you here, but that is one which would show you the kind of thing which is very often repeated, and shows you that there really may be a separation in the living person between his consciousness and his physical body, that that body may show itself as a phantasm, as they call it, to a friend at a distance; and if you want a very large number of instances you can easily refer to *The Phantasms of the Living,* by Mr. Gurney. I ought to say that most of these experiments, or many of them, have been made by the Psychical Research Society, therefore with extreme care, and with very scrupulous observation. To that extent many of them, where they are dealing with those otherwise verified, may throw a good deal of light on these abnormal conditions. The next case I take is a very ordinary one—I mean in a very ordinary man: a change of personality. The man was Mr. Bourne, and he was a kind of traveller, apparently a small trader. He had been ill on several occasions and had fallen into a fit, in one of which it is said he used a very blasphemous expression— but that is really not a very important part of the story. He disappeared one day, having left his home, riding to a neighbouring place to which he went. The horse was left there, but the man had disappeared, and after some three weeks, the wife of the man, knowing where he had been going to, went after him to look for him, and recovered the horse, but could not find a trace of the man. Two weeks later Mr. Ansel Bourne arrived at Norristown, Pa., about February 1, 1887, two weeks after his disappearance from Providence, Rhode Island. There he was Mr. A. J. Brown. He rented a storeroom at 252, East Main Street, from Mr. Pinkston Earle, and divided the room into two by means of curtains. The rear portion of the room he filled with furniture and used as a general living apartment, not only sleeping there, but preparing his own meals there also. The front portion of the room he stocked with notions—whatever they may be—toys, confectionery, etc. These he purchased and paid for in Philadelphia, which he visited each week for the purpose of replenishing his stock. Then he put a sign on the window: "A. J. Brown." The room he rented was part of the house, and he paid his rent for it and went on selling his goods. He was very punctual in the cleaning of his store and attended the Methodist Church on Sunday, and in every way was just an ordinary, normal, quiet person. No one thought he was suffering under any trouble or from any disease. One night he heard an explosion—that is his own explanation—like a gun or a pistol, and waking he noticed that the bed he was in was not like the bed he had been accustomed to sleep in. He noticed the electric light opposite his windows. He rose and pulled away the curtains and looked out on to the street. He felt very weak, and thought he had been drugged. His next sensation was that of fear, knowing that he was in a place where he had no business to be. He feared arrest as a burglar, or possible injury. He says that this was the only time in his life he ever feared a policeman. The last thing he could remember before waking was seeing the Adams's express wagons at the corner of the street in Providence, where he had been, and then he met his landlord, whom he did not know, and a conversation actually took place. "Mr. Earle opened it and said: 'Good morning, Mr. Brown.' Mr. Brown: 'Where am I? Mr. Earle: 'You're all right.' Mr. B.: 'I'm all wrong. My name is not Brown. Where am I?' Mr. E.: 'Norristown.' Mr. B.: 'Where is that?' Mr. E.: 'In Pennsylvania.' Mr. B.: 'What part of the country?' Mr. E.: 'About seventeen miles west of Philadelphia.' Mr. B.: 'What time in the month is it?' Mr. E.: 'The 14th.' Mr. B.: 'Does time run backwards here? When I left home it was the 17th.' Mr. E.: '17th of what?' Mr. B.: '17th January.' Mr. E.: 'It's the 14th of March.'"

Well, there is a very natural conversation. You can see exactly the puzzle of the man and so absolutely commonplace. Nothing there in the very least, one would say, supernatural—the ordinary trader having a fit and changing his personality. There are numbers of those in two great volumes like this. I have only picked out, as I said, four cases, because they are very different and show how wide a range of changes you may find. Then you have one—I am going to take the most remarkable one last of all—in which a woman goes through three states of consciousness. In the first one she is extremely stupid, dull and melancholy, and she was found one morning, long after her habitual time for rising, in a profound sleep from which they could not wake her. She slept for twenty hours and then was awakened. Her memory had gone. She was like a being for the first time ushered into the world. All of the past that remained with her was the faculty of the remembrance of a few words and those seemed to be as purely instinctive as the wailings of an infant. The words she uttered were connected with no ideas in her mind. She had to learn to read over again, bit by bit. She had also to learn to write. Her brother, sisters, parents and friends were not recognised or acknowledged as such by her; she had never seen them before—never known them. To the scene surrounding her she was a perfect stranger : the house, the forest, the hills, the vales, the streams, all were novelties; but the most curious thing is—it is rather a long account—her character was entirely changed. Instead of being dull, melancholy, stupid, she was very alert, very joyous and very adventurous. She was in a rather wild place in the country where there were wild animals in the neighbouring woods. She had not the slightest fear of any one of them. She called them—when they were bears, for instance—hogs, and she was told that the bears were very dangerous. She said: "They are only great hogs—I don't care for them " ; and so much was that the case, that she came in very proud one day, when she had seen "a great black hog" and stated that the hog had become frightened of her instead of her running away from the hog. She said: "I got on my horse and rode on." Well, this went on for a few weeks. She had another change. She had another long sleep. She awoke and was herself again, and recognised all the people around her, and changed her disposition back to the one that she had before. Then she under-went another change, and she came back to the first character that she had been in the second stage that she had had, and the third stage was a kind of intermingling of the two. She became thoughtful, quiet, no longer too joyous or noisy, and in that stage she remained for twenty-five years.

Well, there you have certainly a very remarkable case of three changes, the third being a kind of mingling, as it were, of the two, all in the same body.

Now the fourth case is by far the most remarkable, because it is the inhabiting of the body, not by another human being, but by the soul of a person who had died long before; and I have kept that to the last because it was the most remarkable of these. The child was born in a family named Vennum, and she was named Lurancy—I ask you to remember the name, because it got shortened into Rancy, by which she was always called. In the place where she was born there lived another family named Roff. She was taken away by her parents, who moved three months after she was born. They travelled about for a considerable time, and finally they went back near to the place where they had originally lived. The Roffs were still there, and had lost a daughter named Mary, three months before the Vennums returned to the neighbourhood. Now she was in no way a peculiar child, quite he6.lthy up to the time when she was seventeen years of age. The only illness she had was a slight attack of measles. Then a great change came over her, and she heard her name called at night, "Raney, Rancy," and she complained to her mother that there were persons in her room. The mother then slept in her room with her because she was afraid. Four years after the attack of measles she had a fit, and these fits or trances went on for a whole year, and in some of those she said that she went to Heaven, and that she had there met different people—caught up in a kind of ecstasy apparently—and there she met a girl called Mary. When one of these fits came upon her, her friends wanted her put into a lunatic asylum. The parents resisted, and then they asked, might they bring a particular Dr. Stevens, and when he came into the room she was crouched up by the stove in the position of an old hag, whom she called Hogan; and he, talking with her, suggested that she should come out of the fit, and said she was occupied by an evil spirit and that she had better try to get a better control. She then said that she would like to have as a control Mary Roff, whom she had seen in Heaven. Remember that she had left the place when three months old, and Mary Roff had died three months before her family returned. However, her wish was fulfilled, and the very next day after that, Mary, who had told her in Heaven that she would like to come back to her own family, took possession of her. As soon as this happened, Mary, who had appeared, did not know any of the surroundings in which she found herself; when she said that her name was Mary Roff, they at once thought of their friends in the place. Mr. Roff himself was present during the day, and he said that his daughter Mary Roff had been in Heaven twelve years, adding: "Certainly let her come." He also said: "We will be very glad to have her home again." Well, the next day they took her to Mr. Roff's home and she recognised all the people there. To the father and the mother she said that she was Mary. She told them incidents of her own childhood. She mentioned that she had cut her arm with a knife and had fainted, and that she had had mania after it, and then she said that she had got better again, again got worse and died. It was in February, 1878, that she became the controller, as they called her, of the other girl, Rancy. Then they tried all kinds of experiments to prove her. They found that she recognised things that she played with in her childhood. One day a velvet head-dress that Mary used in the last year before she died was put on the hat-stand and nothing was said about it, to see if she would recognise it. The moment she came into the room she approached the stand, and said: "Oh, there is my head-dress I wore when my hair was short." She then asked: "Where is my box of letters?" and added: "Have you got them yet?" Mrs. Rolf replied: "Yes, Mary, I have some of them," and she at once got the box with the letters in it. As Mary began to look at them she said: "Oh, ma, there is a collar I tatted. Ma, why did you not show to me my letters and things before?" The collar had been preserved among the relics of the lamented child as one of the beautiful things her fingers had wrought. Then suddenly Mary departs, and Raney assumes again the possession of her body. She remembered that Mary had promised to come, but did not remember anything that had happened to Mary after she had come. She married; some years afterwards Mary came back. The whole story is a very long one, but I have given you the gist of it exactly. Now there is a great deal of discussion naturally over that, but there are many other similar cases of the change of personality. What really takes place? The Spiritualists would tell you that it was a spirit from the other world that had wanted to come back and take, the girl's body. That is rejected by the experimenters. Apparently they have their own idea of the change of personality, and they say that it is the coming up from the unconscious of a group of memories and emotions which asserts itself in the body and that this seems to have been a case of what they call dual personality. Now the only way that you can make up your minds on this is by reading, as I have read, a fair amount of literature on the subject. That last story is so unusual to ordinary persons that it is probably rejected by very many as incredible; but if you read a very large number of stories of that kind your incredulity begins to lessen; and one reason why I am conversant with these various books, and older stories as well, is that I went in for a number of experiments myself before I was convinced of the survival of the individuality after death. It was one of the stages which led me from scientific materialism into Theosophy, because in Theosophy I found a rational explanation. Now, frankly, I cannot see any proof of this idea of a personality that disintegrates into a number of groups, of which one or another turns up from time to time without apparently any particular reason. It is not a satisfactory explanation of a thoroughly intelligent change of the kind described above, spoken of beforehand, taking place when it was announced that it would take place, leaving again after a certain time, also announced. I did not tell you that the child went to those she called her parents in the second condition, and went to them because she had to go away again; but you can find numbers of those stories. You see at once that my theosophical studies make it easy for me in this case to realise the use of a body by two persons, because a theosophical explanation is perfectly rational; it can be verified by those who have developed powers of clairvoyance, and they are not very difficult to develop, and can be tested over and over again when you have practised these things, by going to the place where one of the personalities is and knowing where the other is at the same time. You must remember—I would ask you to remember, if you think that on these matters I speak positively as to the possibilities—that I have been practising Yoga for something like thirty-seven years, and that is a long time. It is not like being a beginner, when you may be very often deceived. If one has been practising steadily day by day for many years and going through stage after stage of extension of consciousness, it is not so unnatural after all that one can speak out of one's own knowledge, just as an expert in any other science would say what he knew by his own experiments, whether people believed him or not; and you may also realise why I have so strongly protested, as I said in my first lecture, against the identification of a particular body when its inhabitant is One of those supreme Beings, the One we speak of as the World-Teacher, or the Christ.

Now I do not say that these things ought to convince you; I do say that they are worthy of your study; and I do say that anyone who laughs at the whole thing only shows his ignorance of what modern psychology has done along these very peculiar lines. That has not been my own line of study, except for a short time, when I became convinced that a purely materialistic theory could not be held in the face of the evidence. That was a very long time ago. Since then one has studied this along other lines, has learned how to put off one's own body, has learned how to travel in the subtler body to other places, has learned the various constituents of the different bodies and learned to handle them, as it were, as mere instruments of consciousness. And I shall try in the last lecture on this subject to put before you that other line of investigation which you will find both in East and in West in which the knowledge may be gained by those who are willing to pay the price, who have the patience to investigate, who have the courage to go through long periods of time when the efforts seem to be useless, in the conviction that what others have done in the past may be done in the present, if those who try are willing to take the ancient narrow way, to follow out that teaching of a great Upanishad: "Awake! arise! Seek the great Teachers and attend, for the path is narrow, verily it is narrow, narrow as the edge of a razor."

LECTURE IV

FRIENDS:—

During this course of lectures you may remember that the first was devoted to the more general idea of the coming of a World-Teacher. The second and the third have been dealing with the psychological evidence—first from the East and then from the West—as to the possibility of a change of personality in the human body. You may remember that as far as the eastern psychology was concerned there was no difficulty in the mind of the people; where that psychology is the one recognised practically by all, there was no difficulty in the way of conceiving such a change in the dweller in the body. The ideas there are so full and so clear really in their detail, that that change of the tenant in a body does not strike the ordinary Indian as anything specially remarkable. When we come to the western psychology, it is only comparatively lately that a psychology founded on experiment has led people to consider the possibility of such a change in the tenant of a human body, and to look for explanation of some of the obscurer conditions of the human consciousness to that possibility of change.

Now it is clear that every great religion in the world believes in and teaches the fact of the communication between our physical world and the worlds invisible: communication that may take place on the direct initiative of one in the invisible worlds, but that may also be started by those in our physical world who are ready to undergo the practice of Yoga, whether in East or West. In the East those practices are, as you know, laid down in extreme detail, and a comparatively considerable number of people devote their lives to such practices, with a view to putting an end to what the Buddhist calls "the being bound to the wheel of births and deaths". The great eastern religions, of course, all accept reincarnation as the reason for the evolution in humanity, and to them the gradual accumulation of faculty and of power lies at the root of their thought as to the possibility of a man quickening his evolution. When he has already reached a certain stage in that evolution where the mind has been highly developed, they consider then that it is possible for such a person by a certain course of life and certain definite practices to very much quicken evolution and reach human perfection without going through the long series of reincarnations which otherwise are necessary before the human being can become perfect so far as this world is concerned. One who has reached that point is spoken of by the Buddhists as "one who has no more to learn", meaning by that phrase that this world can do nothing more for him in the way of his growth; and then he only remains in the world if it be his own free will to do so, in order to help his younger brethren also to develop more rapidly and so to reach what they call Liberation—the same idea as you find in the writings of the early Fathers of the Christian Church, only they speak of it as "salvation". The word "salvation", of course, in modern times and mediaeval times, has taken on a very different meaning. In the primitive writers you will find phrases occurring about the continual births and the continual deaths and continual resurrections, until the person reaches the stage of salvation.

Looking, then, for a moment at the various lines of thought that we have been pursuing, there are still, we shall find, some points more scattered in their nature, but I think of great interest, throwing light on some of these processes of swifter evolution and enabling us to understand how it is that there may be living on the physical earth, as far as their life is concerned, beings who have reached the perfection of humanity, who are superhuman, supermen—which is the modern phrase, used in a rather different sense, however—who are voluntarily remaining in physical bodies in order that they may, as I said, assist their younger brethren to quicken their evolution. That has always been regarded as being carried out by what is called "entering upon the Path", a path which has been compared, as many of you know, to the swift climb straight up the mountain side, instead of following all the curves of the road that wind round and round the mountain, escaping the steepness of the direct ascent.

We find in looking at this question that there are two classes of people who are recognised, who seek to quicken their evolution for different reasons and by different methods. One of those methods is usually spoken of as Mysticism, the other as Occultism. Perhaps in the minds of a good many there is confusion between the two, but the two have a different immediate object and also a very different method. The object of the Mystic is to find the way to direct union with God. He does not trouble himself very much about the invisible worlds as such, he is not curious as to their inhabitants, as to the nature of the existences that may be found there; he has one definite point before him, that union with, or merging in, the Divine Life, which will enable him to realise the divinity of his own nature by the direct union which he brings about in a special fashion.

Now, leaving for the moment the eastern way aside, you will find the most exact directions, scientific in their nature, carefully worked out, adapted to this definite end, in the fairly voluminous Roman Catholic literature on the subject You must remember that the Roman Catholic Church has always had in its possession a large amount of knowledge as to both the mystical and the occult methods of the quicker evolution of man. As regards Occultism, while its goal is also the knowledge of God, it seeks to know by personal development, by in-dividual development also, the way in which the invisible worlds—invisible to the body—may be reached by a man still normally living in the body, so that he becomes familiar with their phenomena, so that death ceases to be to him an object of fear or even of curiosity, because he has learned how to penetrate, while still in connection with the mortal body, those so-called "invisible worlds", and to study them by the evolution of the higher senses connected with the bodies of finer matter that he wears, as all of us, of course, wear them. In the Roman Catholic literature, then, so far as Occultism is concerned, it has been kept a very rigid secret, and that is one of the reasons why that Church, speaking generally, is hostile to the Theosophical teaching. They think that it makes the knowledge of those invisible states too common to be either wise or safe for the people at large, and they (while they, many of them, possess the knowledge) very carefully keep it from the reach of the laity. It is known in many of the stricter Orders of monks and nuns, but in both those cases it is less the occult way than the mystic that is pursued in the monastery or the nunnery; and I do not know of any literature, except that of the Hindus, and to some extent of the Buddhists, which gives so precise an idea, has subjected the whole of the question to so rigid an examination, as you may find in some of the literature of the Roman Catholic Church on the subject. They recognise very, very fully the risks of the development, either by Mysticism or by Occultism, at the present stage of human evolution; and some of you who have read some of the histories of the Saints of the Roman Catholic Communion will be aware of the discouragements that surrounded their earlier steps in the direction of mystic attainment, and that when any nun or any monk began to have anything in the nature of communication with the higher worlds it was rigidly discouraged, in some cases very great pressure being put upon the person in order to induce him or her to give up the particular line on which they were entering. It was felt, and felt wisely, to some extent at least, that there were very many dangers along that road—dangers of self-deception, dangers of deception by outside powers, the likelihood of development perhaps of what was called conceit or spiritual pride, and so on—so that if you take some of the lives of the Saints, as for example S. Teresa and S. John of the Cross and others, you will find that the earliest steps along this path were very, very hard to tread, that their spiritual directors, their confessors, were against such communications being received, or talked about, until they were sure that the person was most thoroughly in earnest and also had faculties and capacities which would enable him to tread the path in safety, despite the dangers with which they realised it was surrounded. And you may find in Roman Catholic literature certain books, most of them written abroad but translated also into English, where you have a distinctly scientific account of the way in which the spiritual faculties, as they are called, ought to be developed and protected at the same time, the steps being fully and very, very carefully marked out, and the discipline imposed exceedingly rigid and severe. Putting those points aside, though they are quite necessary for anyone who is going to endeavour to tread this path of Mysticism, it is because of the way in which the subject was studied, because of the numerous efforts which had been made by philosophers and metaphysicians of the Roman Catholic obedience, that they have traced out with such particularity, such detailed instructions, the path by which the human being can attain that condition of sainthood which enables the Church to accept his right to be recognised, and the whole of the methods that have been used in the attaining of that high position. You will find the stages of that marked out with extreme care. These go under the very general name of "Interior Prayer", for every prayer they develop, or rather divide, into certain definite stages. First, they take the ordinary prayer, which they call the vocal or verbal; then they go on to a higher stage in which love and devotion are very strongly developed by a contemplation of the life of the Christ, and also by intensifying love and devotion to God; and then passing out of these stages into a yet higher one, which finally leads to what they call with great truth, but also remarkable boldness in the West, the deification of man, man becoming God, and they do not shrink from that idea. It is true that the books in which that is developed are not books likely to attract in any way the careless or the thoughtless; they need a certain development, naturally, of the intellect, and also a great purification of the emotions, and those preliminary steps are laid down as necessary for the treading of the path to deification.

Now, in the Protestant countries, this subject has not been stressed. You have—but that has been more, I think, in some of the nonconformist sects—a great stress laid upon religious experience. Very much is said about the communion of the believer with God; the stage of salvation has been very clearly marked out,—according to the particular doctrine, of course, in detail—of whatever might be the body of nonconformist Christians who were really devoting themselves to the higher life; and, as I think I mentioned, Dean Inge, Dean of S. Paul's, has done a great deal by his championship of Mysticism to redeem it from the discredit into which it had fallen very largely in western countries, except in those Roman Catholic lands for the people who led what was called the "religious life", in contradistinction to the "life of the world". I think I mentioned to you the astonishment of *The Times* newspaper when those lectures were delivered, and how *The Times,* which is supposed to know so much about everything, said: "We thought that Mysticism was an exploded superstition, and now we learn that it is the only scientific form of religion." Well, those last words are very accurate, for the standpoint that the Dean took was that the one test of fact that the human being had was the testimony of his own consciousness; that that consciousness was affected by impacts from the outer world; that he could not know the nature of the objects but only the effect that they had upon his consciousness; and that the whole of science was based on experiments which recorded the effect on the human consciousness, the human investigator, of the impacts from the outer world. Then he went on to point to religious experiences, and taking these as summed up in the word "Mysticism," he asked people to realise that the religious experiences were as valid as any other experiences of the human consciousness; that they had to be treated with respect as the basis of all human knowledge; that by the senses, the observations of the senses, the impressions made upon the senses, knowledge of the outer world was acquired, and then that knowledge, worked upon by the mind, enabled the human being to understand, to a large extent, the world in which he lived, and to induce the law of Nature, when the phenomena recorded were sufficient for a basis for induction. Looking at it in that way, naturally, the Dean went on to point out that the people who had experiences coming from the invisible worlds had a right to expect respect for those experiences, seeing that the effects caused upon consciousness was our only basis of knowledge; and that is a perfectly fair argument, I think, to use. If a person addresses in prayer an invisible Being in whom he believes as God, if he has any answer to that in his consciousness—a certain definite impression made upon it, of uplifting, perhaps, or of joy and of happiness differing from that gained by physical enjoyment and physical objects—then those experiences, constantly repeated, were a sound basis for knowledge, and that the Mystics of the world had the same right to bear testimony to their experiences as had the scientific men to claim that they were able to add to knowledge by their experiments, their investigations, and the working of the mind upon those classes of phenomena. Looking at it in that way, the Dean was really repeating a well-known verse of the *Bhagavad Gita,* which is said to be a Scripture of Yoga, when it is said that a man who had reached the True Knowledge had no more need of the Scriptures than "a man need dig a well in a place overflowing with water".

All the knowledge of the invisible world comes by repeated experiences, experiences brought about by experiments of the individual; and when you have a very, very large number of individuals all bearing testimony to similar experiences, then you are having a basis for knowledge similar to that on which science bases its knowledge of the laws of Nature.

Now, naturally, in considering this question, you will have to use ordinary human knowledge, which is not adapted to mystical experiences. I found, for instance, in a Roman Catholic classic which I was looking over in connection with this particular view of Mysticism—I found it pointed out that the Mystic had experiences through what they were obliged to call the senses, the spiritual senses;

that is to say, that he might see, or hear, or taste, or smell, or feel touch, not from some physical object which appealed to one or other of those senses and impressed it, but by faculties of a similar nature, that is, direct; and that they had no language in which they could express those experiences except the ordinary language based on the knowledge gained through the senses; and so they speak, for instance, of communications, whether coming from Angels, Saints, or from the Divine Being, as "sight", and "hearing". And, it is argued, and I think quite fairly, that where Beings of intelligence communicate their thoughts the one to the other, you must use the human words to describe the similar experience which you find in the physical world, and therefore they use the term "spiritual senses", just as you may remember that Bergson, speaking of Intuition, because it was direct knowledge, spoke of it in terms of Instinct rather than in terms of Mind. And so, indeed, you may find in other thinkers, as where Leibnitz speaks of Intuitive Knowledge; you may remember that in his definition of perfect knowledge, he adds to the more ordinary definition that it must be, to be perfect, it must be intuitive. You have exactly that same idea again in an Indian Scripture where, in speaking of the ego— the soul, if you prefer that word—it is said, that "His nature is knowledge"; that the knowledge does not come by reasoning, either deductive or inductive, that it presents itself with a completeness like that with which an object of the senses presents itself to the particular sense to which it is addressed; that it is that direct knowledge of Truth because, as the nature of the individual is knowledge, he can tell false suggestions in the same kind of way that a musician detects false notes. The musician does not bother about the number of vibrations that go to make up a note; lie may or may not know anything about that: he knows the falsity of the note by his sense of hearing, directly that note is struck, without any argument at all, by his sense perception. Well, the Roman Catholic writers point out, as eastern writers point out, that the experience of what you may call "spiritual senses" must be described in sense language, because you have no other language in which to express the result of the experience. A person who has done a great deal of training on the lines of Mysticism may say that "an angel spoke to him", without meaning that his physical ear heard the physical voice of an angel; it might be done in that way if the angel chose to materialise himself—that is, take up physical matter and build it into the much finer matter of the body that he habitually wears; but without that he might communicate the idea to the Mystic, who, by the training of those inner senses, is able to, what he is obliged to call, hear what is said to him by the angel. And you will find very, very many cases of that in reading the lives of the Saints. Sometimes their experiences will be all seeing, in seeing some Being who may have materialised himself for the purpose, just as you may read in the Jewish Scriptures or in the Christian Scriptures, that an angel came and spoke physically to a person in the physical body. You may remember a case in the Jewish Scriptures where an angel said: "As captain of the Lord's host I am come"; or you may think of the case of the Annunciation to the Virgin Mary, when the angel appeared. And there are very many such cases, of course, in those Scriptures, as in all the Scriptures of all the other religions of the world.

It is only very lately, with the progress of experimental science, that you find any doubt expressed really with regard to the fact of worlds which are invisible to the ordinary sight as having their own inhabitants, their own laws, knowledge, and so on.

Looking at it, then, from that standpoint, it is perfectly reasonable, I think, if any of you are interested in this subject, to realise that there is a body of literature available to you, and that if you choose to conform to the laws which are laid down for the student, then you will be able to develop—given a certain capacity to begin with, as in all the sciences—you will be able to develop those powers of communication with worlds invisible. Your emotions will be stirred by the impact from those worlds, and so you may rise into a condition of consciousness far higher than that which you use in the ordinary world of our physical experience. That is a matter on which, if I may say it with all courtesy, opinion only becomes valuable when the person expressing it has acquainted himself with the subject on which he gives his opinion. You would readily agree that there are many statements of scientific men that many of you, like myself, would be entirely unable to verify, because they are based on experiments, many of them somewhat delicate and so dangerous that only a man who is devoting his life to the subject can move in safety in that world into which he is penetrating by his experiments and by the work of his mind on the experiments. You cannot gain knowledge at first hand of the outer worlds unless you are willing either to risk yourself or to take the experiences of those who are familiar with those worlds. Take the case of physical science and the early investigators. How many of them injured themselves physically in their experiments along the line of chemistry I Take the case of the well-known monk who invented gunpowder—not entirely for the benefit of mankind at present—but you may remember he was stretched on the floor of his cell several times, knocked senseless by the explosions which he made in his experiments—he lost an eye, one or two fingers, to say nothing of being made unconscious on several occasions. Those are the dangers that inevitably follow the investigator among unknown laws and unknown substances, when you begin to mingle them together to produce the unknown thing for which you are searching. Hence, every sensible person, when he follows a dangerous line of practice, learns from experts in that line, in order that he may not injure himself or others. Is it, then, surprising that the science of the soul, of that which raises man so far above the ordinary members of the animal kingdom—is it surprising that the science of the soul should have its laws, its experts, its dangers? and have you any right to form an opinion on the statements of the experts, unless you have know-ledge of your own, which enables you to estimate the value of the experiments they have made and the results which they have laid down? It seems to me the irrationality is on the other side, the pretence at having an opinion worth expressing on a subject that you have not studied at all. And after all, there are a good many experiments that you might make, not attended with danger, but which would be very much to your general improvement of health, strength, and power of thought.

Looking, then, at the subject from that point, for a moment, let us realise that in this great body of literature on the practice of these various divisions of prayer as they are all called—one of them is meditation, and another control of the emotions, and so on—you have really a scientific literature dealing with worlds which are not normally known; and then when you look back into ancient literature you come across one particular institution which every religion has at its beginning and in its earlier years. Some of them have kept it on to the present time, and the great truths on which it is founded are existing still and can be proved if you care to pay the price.

Now in trying to follow a very rough outline, of course, of this line of thought, you might direct your attention first of all to certain allusions to what are called "the Mysteries" in all the old literatures of the world. The Mysteries were known so far as the fact that they existed. The minor mysteries, or the lesser mysteries, were very largely schools of thought as to the physical world, based on investigations that were made by those who had devoted themselves largely to the investigation of the laws of our world. But those who showed special aptitude for philosophical, metaphysical, and religious thought, they might pass on into the higher Mysteries, the greater Mysteries, and on these for a moment I must pause. Now the true Mysteries have existed from the dawn of humankind down to the present day. The dawn of humankind is very, very far back, as you know, in the recesses of the unknown. Fragments are brought up from time to time. We know, of course, those Mysteries played a very great part, not only with regard to the teaching of morality, which was the business rather of religion, but with the facts on which the religion was founded, and you will remember that the Pharaoh of Egypt was one who, while monarch of the country, was also deeply versed in the Mysteries. Those Mysteries gradually became degraded as time went on. Originally, as they still exist, they are great expansions of consciousness, under the instruction and the guardianship of men who have become perfect in their humanity. Those expansions of consciousness take place in definite stages; four of them lead up to that liberation or salvation of which I spoke, the escape from the power of death. Then beyond that, still higher Mysteries are to be found, which deal with the Inner Government of the world, that Inner Government which is ever watching over the world and taking advantage of every opportunity in which man may be helped and evolution may not be retarded in its course. Those, then, exist as they have ever existed. The thought of them was revived in the time of the elder amongst us when the Theosophical Society came into the world and Madame H. P. Blavatsky began to teach about the existence of these superhuman Men, and of the knowledge that They could give to the world as to the higher life. They were asked on one occasion, one of Them,, whether They would not help the science of the time—Sir William Crookes was one of the members of the Society when it was founded, and he was helped, to some extent—but the answer to the general question was: "We will never help the science of the West until the social conscience has developed to a higher point than it has yet attained." And I think if you look at the progress of the science of late years you will realise how wise and merciful that answer was; for in the investigations of modern science, as you know, many of the greatest of those in scientific knowledge, many of those men are devoting their time to finding out more terrible methods whereby man can destroy his fellow-man: poison gases far more horrible than those used in the last fratricidal war, poison gases so terrible that they tell us that if a fleet of aeroplanes armed with it were sent over this great city of London and dropped bombs it would be, in a few hours, a heap of ruins and filled with the corpses of every man, woman and child living within the devastated area. Such a science is not beneficent, it is not even human, but criminal; and while men use their faculties for such purposes you cannot expect that that Inner Government of the world, ruled by compassion and wisdom, will help to unveil any of the secrets which might be used for purposes so alien from love and brotherhood: They cannot stop the course of the evolution of the human mind, They can put obstacles sometimes in the way, but they cannot entirely stop it; They must let the civilisation kill itself, if that is the way of the science of the time, and then once more man will have to climb up again out of ignorance, as have perished the civilisations of the past when they became a source of misery to mankind instead of being beneficent and uplifting. But other knowledge to a very, very large extent was given through Their chosen messenger, and she down here took pupils and taught them much of what she knew, so that when she passed away others were left, who could carry on similar investigations and help others to tread the path that leads to Life Eternal. And so, it having been a command given many centuries ago that in the last quarter of a century help should be given to the West to make progress, so it has come to pass that the deeper knowledge of spiritual progress has been opened again along the ancient narrow way, and many are treading that ancient path, many are learning some of the supposed secrets of the invisible world; and that is the study of what is known as Occultism, as distinguished from Mysticism. In Mysticism the union with God which makes the saint carries him away from earth; Occultism is the path that leads to still remaining in the physical body, so as to be able to help the younger brethren also to tread the path that leads to Life. And so we have, looking back into the past, we have these Mysteries, and the real, the greatest Mysteries still exist; so that those of you who will make the necessary sacrifice may learn to pass them yourselves, as some of us have done.

Looking at it, then, in that way, you may realise that it is possible to gain knowledge of these "spirit worlds" as they are called—I would rather say, invisible worlds; they are worlds of finer matter, not all of them spiritual, but intellectual and rising up to the spiritual finally.

Now you have had a great deal all over the world of what is known as Spiritualism, and I will just say in passing that there is this profound difference between the communication gained along the line of Spiritualism and the knowledge gained along the line of Occultism, and it is this: in Spiritualism you have what is called a medium, a person of a certain sensitive nature and also with one peculiarity, which has been very fully investigated of late years, the power of giving up the etheric, much of the etheric part of the body, and also some of the liquids and gases, and even the dense physical slightly, so that someone from the other side of death, drawing upon the medium, may be able what is called "to materialise" himself, and teach or speak through that materialisation to the sitters at the séance; that is to say, when a person has passed into a higher world of subtler matter, you can give him the opportunity of densifying himself again to communicate with the people who meet together for that purpose. Now many of us think that that is not the best way of winning communication with the worlds of finer matter; that as everyone of us has bodies consisting of the matter of those worlds—as I was putting to you in one of these lectures, there is what is called "mind stuff", in which we think; "emotion stuff", in which our emotions express themselves; much as our activities express themselves through the dense muscles and nerves—there is a certain draining of the life and strength of the medium, which seems to some of us unjustifiable. And also you can thus only reach those who have not gone very far up in the higher worlds, and most usually reach those who are in the lower strata of those worlds, and who tell you their own experiences certainly; but you cannot take that as general, as regards the whole of the worlds in which your own bodies live normally, definitely and capable of further evolution. Suppose, then, that you learn to do of your own free will, at any time, what you do every night in sleep; suppose your consciousness then goes out into what has been called the dream world, as I told you many experiments have been made upon that; suppose you go into the deeper state of trance, many experiments have been made upon that; and suppose you learn to develop those bodies to work in their own worlds apart from your dense physical body, then you are just like travellers going into an unknown country and observing all the things which surround you: you can communicate with the objects, you can see the objects made in the matter of those worlds, and as you gradually train yourself along these lines there is nothing to prevent your then making observations as accurately, and more accurately than the ordinary scientist can make his observations by the aid of spectroscope and microscope. There you have what I know sounds as an assertion only, but I would ask you to remember that in the literature, the best, the most magnificent literature that you have from the nations of the past, these Mysteries are spoken of, spoken of by men like Plato, and not one of you, I am sure, would deny to him the possession of a remarkable intellectual genius. He speaks of how they had their knowledge of immortality from the things they learned in those Mysteries, how they came to understand death and the life carried on on the other side of death. And you may find such references as these made in many, many books from the past. There is other evidence of the past civilisations from our antiquarians and archaeologists, who have dug through part of the crust of the earth and unburied the buried fragments of those ancient times. And when you begin to examine into these, you may, if you like, trace out those great Mysteries that went to make Egypt what she was, seeing, as I think I mentioned to you, some of the gestures that are used in the paintings that are also used in modern Masonry. You may find that the Mysteries pass through several stages—a stage of drama, where ordinary human beings act out as a drama the states on the other side of death. You may read of some of the gloomy caverns that have been discovered, caverns through which the would-be Initiate was led, where attempts were made to frighten him, where they tried to scare him back, and so on. And you may even know that of modern Freemasonry it is said to be a system of allegories illustrated by symbols. Now what do the symbols mean? What lies behind the allegories? Probably many of you are acquainted with these allegories and symbols. Do they tell nothing to you of the realities which are hidden behind them? Is it a mere almost waste of time that so many men amongst you give to your Masonic duties? And when you answer questions that are asked, and use the words I have just quoted as an explanation of Masonry, do you not sometimes wish to know what lies behind these allegories, the truths of the world invisible which were put into allegories, which were put into symbols, in order that for all time vessels might remain into which the spiritual knowledge might be poured when men were found who were ready to sacrifice for the winning of it, and who would do in fact what Masonry does in symbol? The whole of that is not mere folly, mere childish dressing up, mere foolish gestures; they are the vessels of great realities of the invisible worlds, which, as Plato told you, assured those who were Initiates of their own immortality on the other side of death. And it has been kept alive through all the ages that so, when the spiritual truths again are proclaimed, they may be recognised in the symbolism which has kept them safe from persecution for many ages. And then some of you may begin to realise that these ideas are true and not false, and that men of to-day, as men in the past, may penetrate into the worlds invisible to physical eyes, and may there learn the secrets of those worlds which will quicken their evolution, which will enable them to become more useful to their fellow-men, and finally to join that great band of the Guardians and Saviours of the world, from which sometimes, at long intervals, comes out a Messenger to see whether the world has grown far enough to realise and love His message. And you, looking back to the Christ, that last greatest Messenger of the White Lodge, you know how He taught brotherhood, how He taught sacrifice, how He taught love, and how He taught that the greatest among you is he that doth serve. And yet, what is Christendom to-day but a field of warring nations, and warring classes within every nation, a struggle of class against class, of capital against labour, and labour against capital? Where is the brotherhood which is trampled underfoot in the civilisation that dares to take the name of Christendom, and tramples upon every principle the Christ taught of love and service to our fellow-men? That is the position you have to face to-day. Your statesmen cannot cure it; your scientists only make it worse. Is it any wonder, then—if the old proverb be true that "Man's defeat is God's opportunity"—that again from that Inner Government there should come forth that same great Teacher to a world two thousand years older than when He trod last the streets of its cities, to try if that message re-proclaimed *and lived* may give the basis of a better civilisation where men will really be brothers, where there will be opportunity of knowledge and of happiness? For only by a blunder of translation they have spoken of His coming as the end of the world. By a blunder of translation they have put Him far away, in a far-off heaven, instead of His living in the world He loves and serves. And if one of the lowest of His servants tell you that she knows, because she heard Him say it, that He is coming again as the Helper of the world, surely you might at least realise that the question is a grave one. And if you want to study it, the way to you is open. But I would pray to you, for your own sakes, do not ridicule the idea, do not scoff, for in scoffing you are scoffing at the Christ Himself—He the ever-loving Saviour, He the Elder Brother of our race, He who should be born in the hearts of every one of you, and growing in you to the measure of the full stature of the Christ. At least, if you do not believe, do not encourage the degradation by ridicule of that great message of His coming. Reject Him again when He comes if you will, and then let your civilisation go down as others, which have gone before.

Printed in Great Britain
by Amazon

38547481R00030

Books in the Life Writing Series Published by Wilfrid Laurier University Press

Haven't Any News: Ruby's Letters from the Fifties
Edited by Edna Staebler
with an Afterword by Marlene Kadar
1995 / x + 165 pp. / ISBN 0-88920-248-6

"I Want to Join Your Club": Letters from Rural Children, 1900-1920
Edited by Norah L. Lewis
with a Preface by Neil Sutherland
1996 / xii + 250 pp. (30 b&w photos) / ISBN 0-88920-260-5

And Peace Never Came
Elisabeth M. Raab
with Historical Notes by Marlene Kadar
1996 / x + 196 pp. (12 b&w photos, map) / ISBN 0-88920-281-8

Dear Editor and Friends: Letters from Rural Women of the North-West, 1900-1920
Edited by Norah L. Lewis
1998 / xvi + 166 pp. (20 b&w photos) / ISBN 0-88920-287-7

The Surprise of My Life: An Autobiography
Claire Drainie Taylor
with a Foreword by Marlene Kadar
1998 / ISBN 0-88920-302-4
xii + 268 pp. (8 colour photos and 92 b&w photos)

Memoirs from Away: A New Found Land Girlhood
Helen M. Buss/Margaret Clarke
1998 / xvi + 153 pp. / ISBN 0-88920-314-8

The Life and Letters of Annie Leake Tuttle: Working for the Best
Marilyn Färdig Whiteley
1999 / xviii + 150 pp. / ISBN 0-88920-330-X

Marian Engel's Notebooks: "Ah, mon cahier, écoute"
Christl Verduyn, editor
1999 / viii + 576 pp. / ISBN 0-88920-333-4

Be Good, Sweet Maid: The Trials of Dorothy Joudrie
Audrey Andrews
1999 / xvi + 276 pp. / ISBN 0-88920-334-2